Can We Feed the World
Without Destroying It?

Global Futures Series

Mohammed Ayoob, *Will the Middle East Implode?*
Jacqueline Bhabha, *Can We Solve the Migration Crisis?*
Christopher Coker, *Can War be Eliminated?*
Howard Davies, *Can Financial Markets be Controlled?*
Jonathan Fenby, *Will China Dominate the 21st Century?* 2nd ed
Andrew Gamble, *Can the Welfare State Survive?*
David Hulme, *Should Rich Nations Help the Poor?*
Joseph S. Nye Jr., *Is the American Century Over?*
Tamara Sonn, *Is Islam an Enemy of the West?*
Dmitri Trenin, *Should We Fear Russia?*
Jan Zielonka, *Is the EU Doomed?*

Eric Holt-Giménez

Can We Feed the World Without Destroying It?

polity

The right of Eric Holt-Giménez to be identified as Author of this Work has been asserted in accordance with the UK Copyright, Designs and Patents Act 1988.

First published in 2018 by Polity Press
Reprinted: 2019, 2020

Polity Press
65 Bridge Street
Cambridge CB2 1UR, UK

Polity Press
101 Station Landing
Suite 300
Medford, MA 02155, USA

ISBN-13: 978-1-5095-2200-2
ISBN-13: 978-1-5095-2201-9(pb)

A catalogue record for this book is available from the British Library.

Library of Congress Cataloging-in-Publication Data

Names: Holt-Giménez, Eric, author.
Title: Can we feed the world without destroying it? / Eric Holt-Giménez.
Description: Cambridge, UK ; Medford, MA : Polity Press, 2018. | Series:
    Global futures | Includes bibliographical references and index.
Identifiers: LCCN 2018019582 (print) | LCCN 2018020355 (ebook) | ISBN
    9781509522040 (Epub) | ISBN 9781509522002 (hardback) | ISBN 9781509522019
    (pbk.)
Subjects: LCSH: Food supply--Environmental aspects. | Agriculture and
    state--Environmental aspects. | Sustainable agriculture. | Hunger.
Classification: LCC HD9000.5 (ebook) | LCC HD9000.5 .H65 2018 (print) | DDC
    338.1/9--dc23
LC record available at https://lccn.loc.gov/2018019582

Typeset in 11 on 15 pt Sabon by
Servis Filmsetting Ltd, Stockport, Cheshire
Printed and bound to in the United States by LSC Communications, Inc.

For further information on Polity, visit our website: politybooks.com

Contents

Acknowledgments   vi

1 The Politics, Power, and Potential of Food   1
2 Hunger in a World of Plenty   10
3 Food, Environment, and Systems Change   40
4 Who *Can* Feed the World Without
   Destroying It?   88

Further Reading   119
Notes   124

Acknowledgments

Many thanks to all of the writers and researchers of food and agriculture who did the research upon which this book is based. The board of directors of Food First supported me with a much-needed sabbatical, during which time I turned a loose collection of chapters written in a year's worth of spare moments into a full manuscript. My heartfelt thanks to the Food First staff, who filled in for me while I was away. Ilja Van Lammeren helped me draft the initial outline for this book, the editors at Polity provided many helpful suggestions, and four anonymous reviewers helped bring the manuscript to press with their constructive comments. My wife and companion Leonor Hurtado provided invaluable support and encouragement throughout the writing process. Thanks to all of you for helping strike another blow against the injustices that cause hunger.

1

The Politics, Power, and Potential of Food

How times have changed. Fifty years ago, few doubted that a combination of high-yielding hybrids, chemical fertilizers, powerful pesticides, extensive irrigation, and big machinery would make hunger a thing of the past. We had but to spread the "Green Revolution" around the world and modern technology would give us a cornucopian abundance of food – as long as we controlled population growth.

Now, we're not so sure. In some places and for some people, the ability to produce enough food remains life's central challenge. But when we look at the global food system, we see a whole new set of problems more related to overproduction than to the challenges associated with scarcity of food. For example, chronically low prices paid to farmers, inordinately high levels of food waste, and the repurposing of grains and oilseeds for feed and fuel rather than for food are all a reflection of systemic overproduction. The high indices of hunger and malnutrition among the world's peasant farmers are also a reflection of oversupply: large, industrial farms with massive market power are producing vast surpluses and monopolizing land and resources, driving these small farmers into bankruptcy and hunger.

We've gone from questioning our capacity to produce enough food to questioning the way we produce it. Even though the rate of global population growth has leveled off and we are producing more food than ever before, nearly a third of the world's people presently suffer from hunger and malnutrition. Feeding them – and the world's projected population of 10 billion people by 2050 – has become a high-profile challenge for governments, multilateral institutions, relief and development programs, big philanthropy, and even the Fortune 500.

Fears of future famines and widespread malnutrition have unleashed a steady march of initiatives to double food production within a generation. Today, a powerful phalanx of genetic technologies, big data, big farms, and big supermarkets has partnered with governments and multilateral agencies in a global push to end world hunger.

But will producing twice as much food tax the resources of our planet beyond capacity? Our food system's ecological footprint is already alarming. The loss of biodiversity and ecosystem services costs over 10 percent of the world's annual gross product. More than 75 billion tons of fertile soil are lost yearly due to desertification, soil erosion, and soil degradation. Industrial agriculture uses up 75 percent of the world's fresh water and has led to a loss of over 90 percent of the world's agrobiodiversity. Agricultural runoff has created vast eutrophic "dead zones" from the Gulf of Mexico to the Baltic Sea. Are further contamination, loss of habitat, and species extinction inevitable consequences of feeding the world?

Further, as the increase in extreme weather events, the disappearing polar ice cap, and the rising of the seas all make clear, our greenhouse-gas-spewing industrial food system has entered a dangerous negative feedback loop. The way we produce and consume food is undermining our ability to produce food at all.

Food itself has gone from being something that is good for you to something that is often bad for you. In addition to hunger, obesity, pandemics, food poisoning, and diet-related disease have been added to the list of food problems. Because of the ways we produce, process, deliver, and consume it, food abundance has become as troublesome as food scarcity. We've become as worried about the solutions as we are about the problem. The addendum to the question "Can we feed the world without destroying it?" is "and not kill ourselves in the process?"

These questions are all grounded in longstanding frameworks of scarcity – of too many people competing for too few resources. Population expert Paul Ehrlich claims the earth's human population must be reduced by over two-thirds, to 1.5–2 billion, if we are all to live a modern urban lifestyle. But this straight-line resource accounting does not analyze the political-economic nature of the social systems that drive resource consumption, and leads us to the irresolvable ethical dilemma of which eight out every ten people should be eliminated.

Nonetheless, hunger and the depletion of resources are real, as is the expected growth of the planet's population by another 3 billion. But the assumption that scarcity and population growth cause hunger is riddled with contradictions, as is the notion that food production is invariably destructive.

In the 1970s, when one in seven people on the planet were going hungry, fear of planetary "overshoot" framed the international discussions at the Club of Rome, the United Nations (UN), and most of the northern agencies working in the Third World. The conventional, Malthusian wisdom held that the rising global population would eventually eat us out of house and home. Unless we curbed population growth and doubled food production with modern agricultural technologies, the planet and its human inhabitants would be destroyed by billions of empty bellies.

A half-century after these dire predictions, the world economy has generated a massive increase in food and wealth. However, at least one person in every seven is still officially going hungry (the real figure is probably twice that) and, if measured realistically, the numbers of people living in poverty are not falling significantly. But it is not the poor and the hungry who are putting pressure on our food systems and the environment; it is the growing market demand from middle-class consumers in both the Global North and the Global South – consumers whose appetites for grain and soy-fed meat and out-of-season produce are economic pillars of the global food system. While the double specter of overpopulation and scarcity is still prominent in antihunger and environmental discourse, the bane of overconsumption is quietly emerging alongside overproduction as the challenge of our times.

Today, we already produce enough food to feed

10 billion people – that's one-and-a-half times more food than is actually needed to feed every man, woman, and child of the 7.6 billion people presently walking the earth. Nonetheless, depending on the metric, between 1 million and 3 billion people are still going hungry. This is why – we are constantly told – we have to double food production by 2050. Doubling food production within a generation has been a global imperative since the 1960s when the Green Revolution claimed to have saved a billion people from starvation. This claim, inferred from an increase in global food production (though never actually verified on the ground), held that hunger was a problem of underdevelopment to be solved by extending modern technologies offered by Western powers. These assumptions – and the highly lucrative expansion of the agribusiness sector – led people to ignore hunger when it appeared in the midst of wealth, abundance, low-population density, and high productivity, for example in the United States.

The permanent celebration of the technological effectiveness of the Green Revolution, and the constant calls to end global hunger seem contradictory. As late as 2015, the UN announced that the Millennium Development Goals (MDGs) were being met and that we were on track to end hunger and poverty. At the same time, the UN Food and

Agriculture Organization (FAO), while admitting that there was 50 percent more than enough food to feed everyone, insisted that we had to increase our food supply by 70 percent over the next thirty years. What can we make of this? How is it that billions of people are hungry and malnourished even though there is too much food? If we are already overproducing food, how will producing more food end hunger? We never seem to have enough food – even when we produce too much of it. Like the brooms of the Sorcerer's Apprentice, hunger seems to increase each time it is eradicated.

The perpetual calls to end hunger, on the one hand, and to maintain our faith in technological progress, on the other, is a globalized form of cognitive dissonance that avoids addressing the contradiction of hunger in a world caught in the grips of overproduction and overconsumption.

Calls to end hunger routinely avoid distinguishing between need and demand. People are going hungry not because of lack of food, but because they are too poor to buy it. That most of the people suffering from hunger are farmers is a contradiction that is easily missed in the narratives of scarcity, hunger, and technological solutions.

The uneasy question posed in the title of this book, "Can we feed the world without destroying it?" appeals to our emotions and our ethics at the irreducible level of food, humanity, and nature. To answer "no" is to succumb to extinction, or to a cynical future of haves and have-nots, in which a privileged minority eats well and thrives in a lush, green world, while the majority is condemned to bad food and misery in a polluted, climate-ravaged global desert. To say "yes" is to reaffirm our faith in the technological approaches that have helped bring us to the brink of environmental collapse. "Can we feed the world without destroying it?" is a question that – unless interrogated – leads us, quite literally, to a dead end. The critical response of this book is both "No, not the way we are feeding it now" and "Yes, if we make fundamental changes to the food system."

Simply doubling production under the present food system will not end hunger, but – without fundamental changes to how we produce food and distribute wealth – may indeed push our planet beyond its ecological limits and destroy the lives and livelihoods of billions of people. The social and environmental failures of our current food system are the result of an inequitable and extractivist food regime[1] that has been centuries in the making. The technologies, expertise, and resources to feed everyone – without destroying the planet

– have existed for a long time. The real question is: "What is keeping us from feeding the world without destroying it?"

To answer this question, the book addresses not only the agronomy and ecology of food production, but also the political economy of food – that is, the way resources, value, and power are distributed across the entire food system – from farm to fork. This approach uses critical theory and a structural analysis of capitalism to understand who has what, who does what, who gets what, and what they do with it in the food system. The book also focuses on alternatives to the status quo, identifies the barriers to their adoption, and lays out the social and political opportunities for changing the food system – a challenge that embraces both the power of social movements and the imperative of whole systems transformation.

Because we have a capitalist food system, feeding the world without destroying it requires a critical understanding of capitalism. It also requires that we find ways to unleash the tremendous social power within the world's food systems not just to change the way we produce and consume our food, but also to transform society itself. This book aims to contribute to this challenge.

2

Hunger in a World of Plenty

Following a devastating famine in Bangladesh, United States Secretary of State Henry Kissinger, at the 1974 World Food Conference in Rome, famously promised to end child hunger within ten years. World leaders applauded. Even though one in seven people were going hungry worldwide, they had cause for optimism. Following the introduction of the Green Revolution – an international campaign to spread fertilizers, pesticides, and high-yielding grain varieties to farmers throughout the developing world – global food production had dramatically increased. At least 1 billion people, it was claimed, had been saved from starvation. As the twenty-first century approached, global food surpluses and a well-established system for food aid had practically eradicated the scourge of famine from the face of the earth.

But over the next two decades – despite a food increase of 12 percent per capita – the number of hungry people rose from 650 million to 830 million. Following the food price crises of 2008 and 2011, hunger exploded to encompass 1.2 billion people.

Then, in 2013, the United Nations (UN) announced that the number of hungry people was falling. In 2015, the final report of the Millennium Development Goals (MDGs) boldly declared: "Projections indicate a drop of almost half in the proportion of undernourished people in the developing regions."[1] Ending hunger was again within our grasp.

Until it wasn't.

In 2017, the UN's Food and Agriculture Organization (FAO) had to admit that hunger was on the rise: "In addition to an increase in the proportion of the world's population that suffers from chronic hunger (prevalence of undernourishment), the number of undernourished people on the planet has also increased to 815 million, up from 777 million in 2015."[2] The good news on hunger had been short-lived. The devil (as we will later see) was in the counting.[3]

Large numbers of people are hungry – much larger numbers than the official statistics would have you believe. The dominant view is that hunger is due to scarcity, but it's a much more complex problem. In fact, modern-day hunger is a problem of overproduction.

How can too much food cause hunger? To understand this enigma, we need to look at both the market and the production process. Commercial farmers don't produce food to feed people: they produce food to sell on the market, where they compete with other food producers. Whoever can produce the most food at the cheapest price will have the most market power – power to flood markets and push out other producers. When smaller, subsistence farmers who are actually growing most of the world's food go broke, they often go hungry.

This chapter addresses why our food system overproduces, how this is part and parcel of capitalist food production, and how it affects producers, consumers, and the politics of hunger. We'll start with the constantly changing official statistics on the fight against hunger.

Feeding the hungry: enduring myths and slippery statistics

Despite the fact that there is enough food to feed everyone 3,000 calories a day, independent analyses indicate that today over a third of the world is going hungry.[4] That is nearly three times more than the FAO's calculations. How can the numbers be so different?

It turns out that measuring hunger is as contentious as ending it. Behind eroding commitments, the multilateral process for ending hunger is riven with slippage.

At the Rome World Food Summit in 1996, when the leaders from 185 countries reviewed the unmet commitments made at the 1974 World Food Conference, they decided that ending hunger completely was too ambitious. Instead, the Declaration of Rome promised to reduce the total number of hungry people by half – to 420 million by 2015.[5]

Four years later the Millennium Declaration diluted the Rome Declaration's commitment even further from cutting the *total number* of hungry people to reducing the *proportion* of hungry people by half by 2015. Because of the global population increase, this adjustment meant ending hunger for only 296 million people – not 420 million.[6] The MDGs then weakened the target even more by declaring that halving the proportion of hungry people would only apply to developing countries – where population growth is highest.[7] This meant that, globally, even more people would be allowed to go hungry.

The next statistical easing was to backdate the base year from 2000, when the goals were agreed upon, to 1990. This allowed rich Western countries to take into account China's extraordinary accomplishments of the 1990s, in which millions of people were pulled from poverty and hunger – even though China was not part of the Millennium Declaration. It also extended the period of population growth, thus increasing the proportion of people saved from hunger, and allowed the MDGs to claim gains in hunger reduction before the goals were even activated.[8]

This meant that the new MDG for hunger actually increased the "acceptable" number of hungry people in the world from 420 million to 591 million and slowed the rate of hunger reduction from 3.58 percent per year to 1.25 percent per year – down to almost one-third of the original rate.

But that's not all. The UN then decided to change the original numbers used in the 1990 baseline. Twice.

In 1992 the FAO reported that in 1990, 786 million people had gone hungry in the developing world. But ten years later – a year after signing the MDGs – they reassessed and inflated that number to 816 million, thereby allowing them to report a decrease of 30 million more hungry people than would otherwise have been the case.[9]

Then, in 2004 the FAO reported that hunger had increased to 815 million people. Even with the revised calculations, this meant that in four years the number of people going hungry had been reduced by only 1 million. In fact, hunger had actually increased from the original 1990 calculation of 786 million. But the FAO revised the original 1990 figure again, increasing it to 824 million, so hunger appeared to have decreased after all.[10]

Ignoring the global food price crisis

In 2008 the global food price crisis hit, pushing the price of food beyond historic levels and driving more than 150 million people into the ranks of the hungry. The FAO reported a record 1.2 billion hungry people – at a time of record harvests and record corporate profits.[11] Reaching the MDG targets was going to be impossible.

As the MDG's 2015 expiration date approached, the FAO revised the numbers again. In 2012 they announced hunger in the developing world was down from its 2008 record high of 1.2 billion, to 852 million people. This was still higher than their 1990 figure (824 million), meaning the world was getting farther away from the MDG target. So, the

FAO adjusted the 1990 numbers up once again, from 824 million to 980 million. This made it appear that proportional hunger was decreasing: from 23 percent in 1990 to 15 percent in 2012. The 2013 UN report on the MDGs proclaimed: "Progress in reducing hunger has been more pronounced than previously believed, and the target of halving the percentage of people suffering from hunger by 2015 is within reach." Astonishingly, the FAO also stated that "[Our] methodology does not ... fully reflect the effects on hunger of the 2007–08 price spikes ... let alone the recent price increases."[12]

But how could the FAO ignore a food price crisis affecting more than 150 million people?

What is being measured?

The FAO counts people as hungry only when caloric intake becomes inadequate to cover minimum needs for a sedentary lifestyle for over a year. But most hungry people are peasant farmers engaged in demanding physical labor and need up to 3,000–4,000 calories a day – much more than the FAO's "sedentary" minimum caloric threshold. Most of these farmers are women, who are often nursing children and need at least another 500 calories a day.

If we measure hunger at the more accurate (and still conservative) level of calories required for normal activity, we see that 1.5 billion people are hungry (according to an annex in the FAO's own 2012 report), which is twice as many as the UN would have us believe.[13] If we measure hunger at the level of calories required for intense activity, the number of hungry is 2.5 billion.

Though the FAO admits that there are 2.1 billion people suffering as a result of serious vitamin and nutrient deficiencies, it does not count them as being hungry. What the FAO counts for hunger is caloric intake, not actual nutrition. And since the definition of hunger only captures hunger that lasts for more than a year, it does not count someone who is hungry for 11 months out of the year.[14]

In reality, 73 percent of the apparent gains in hunger statistics come from China, most of which occurred during the 1990s, before the MDGs even began. Given that China's infamous "Great Leap Forward" unleashed one of the last major famines of the twentieth century, these gains are extraordinary – and unprecedented in the Western world. Progress against hunger in China was largely the result of land reform, which guaranteed small farmers secure access to land.[15]

2.5 billion hungry

Ending hunger by dint of statistical manipulation is a devastatingly poor substitute for actually ending it.

The MDGs masked, rather than revealed, the true extent of hunger. In reality between 1.5 and 2.5 billion people do not have access to adequate supplies of food – much higher than the 815 million calculated by the FAO in 2017.

After the expiration of the Millennium Development Goals, in 2016 the UN Development Program introduced the Sustainable Development Goals (SDGs).[16] Ending hunger completely by 2030 is the second of seventeen ambitious goals. The good news is that zero can't be statistically manipulated. The bad news is that we are moving away from, not toward, these goals.

The inability of a food regime with $6 trillion in yearly sales to end hunger is a painful reminder of the failure of the Development Decades (1960s–80s) to bring lasting prosperity to the Global South. Despite an impressive half-century of economic growth, and despite the rise of the middle classes in middle-income countries, hunger persists because poverty persists. Admitting our food system is failing would call into question the last thirty years of neoliberal economic policy: free trade agreements, the privatization of public goods, and the deregulation of labor and environmental laws. It would call into question the loudly trumpeted claims by the biotech sector that genetically modified organisms (GMOs) – now nearly twenty-five years on the market – are saving the world from hunger.

Admitting our food system is failing calls into question capitalism itself.

Scarcity: the myth that feeds all others

In the mid-1980s, researchers Frances Moore Lappé and Joseph Collins warned that hunger was not a myth, but that myths keep us from ending hunger.[17] These myths include: that hunger is due to food scarcity and overpopulation, that only industrial agriculture can feed the world (organic and ecological farming can't), and that the free market, free trade, and food aid are the best way to help the hungry. Lappé and Collins still contend that if we recognize these as myths and introduce more democracy into our food system, we can end hunger.[18] This is easier said than done, particularly for the central, and most enduring, myth: scarcity – the myth that is the foundation for all the others.

The scarcity myth is as powerful today as it was fifty years ago. A review of papers and websites from antihunger and development agencies, and of the agrifoods industry, reveal constant calls to increase food production by 60, 70, or even 100 percent by the year 2050 to avoid mass hunger and starvation.

But these calls are based on projections made from econometric models that do not measure food in pounds or calories, but in how many dollars' worth of food will be needed to meet the expected market demand. As the authors of the FAO's original research admit, these are not predictions of need, they are economic projections of demand. They were never intended to become normative targets for ending hunger.[19] Further, econometric forecasts skew projections in favor of meat, a very expensive food. As scientific advisor on the climate and energy program at the Union of Concerned Scientists, Doug Boucher writes: "[This] way of doing the calculations counts meat, and particularly beef, way out of proportion to its calorie or protein content. So that as global diets shift towards more meat as incomes increase, the projection of 'need,' done in dollar terms, will go up."[20] This exercise in economics assumes that the world's middle classes will continue to grow over the next thirty years, thus increasing the demand for meat – and that the resources (primarily water, land and nutrients) will be available to produce it. These are heroic assumptions.

No matter. The mantra of doubling food production is repeated over and again, as if marketing more grain-fed meat to the middle classes will somehow feed the poor. This is supported by a lot of advertising from the chemical, seed, grain, livestock, and feed industries that would have us believe that expansion of their commercial operations responds to a global concern to end hunger.

The persistence of the scarcity myth is due in part to the memory of the planet's 70 million famine-related deaths in the twentieth century. But the sociopsychological power of scarcity is structurally embedded in a capitalist economic system that prioritizes market demand over human needs: a system that suffers periodic crises of overproduction, and actually thrives on scarcity.

Scarcity in capitalist markets occurs when consumer demand exceeds supply, a necessary condition for an increase in the rate of profit. When the opposite happens – supply exceeds demand – markets are saturated and the rate of profit falls. This can result in a "crisis of overproduction," a cyclical occurrence in capitalism in which goods pile up unsold, companies cut back on production, people are laid off, and a recession occurs.

A crisis of overproduction sends smaller firms into bankruptcy. This consolidates production and market power into larger and larger monopoly corporations. When profit margins are reduced, stockholder returns evaporate, leading them to sell off their shares. This can drive mega-mergers – for example, the Dow–DuPont, Syngenta–ChemChina, and Monsanto–Bayer mergers currently under way, which will allow a handful of chemical companies to monopolize the world's commercial seeds. The introduction of new products, technologies, and economies of scale to lower costs and find new efficiencies, along with opening new markets – by force if necessary – must be employed to re-establish scarcity.

The basic tendency in capitalist food systems to overproduce, concentrate capital, and constantly expand is a result of competition. As firms compete, they intensify production, lowering unit costs. This reduces prices, leading to more consumption – and more competition, which leads to more production, until markets are saturated. The steady decline in food prices in the decades leading up to the food price crisis reflects a continuous oversupply of food. Of course, not everyone is getting more food, because hunger is increasing, not decreasing. While it is often portrayed as a problem of distribution and overpopulation, this lack of effective demand simply means that too many people are just too poor to buy all the food being produced. Why are they so poor?

Hunger results from overproduction, not scarcity

Overproduction, not scarcity, characterizes our food system. Over the past half-century, the growth in global food supply has consistently surpassed the need for food by 50 percent. Nonetheless, multilateral development agencies, agribusiness, and many antihunger advocates insist we need to increase global food production dramatically in order to feed a growing global population. Critics of this position point out that we already grow enough food to feed 10 billion people – and yet we still can't end hunger. How is growing more food going to change that?[21]

As much as 70 percent of the world's hungry are farmers, mostly women, who produce over half the world's food on less than 25 percent of the planet's agricultural land.[22] How can they be going hungry? And why are they women? The economic answer is poverty. The systemic answer is patriarchy, exploitation, and dispossession.

Capitalist agriculture has a strong tendency to overproduce. Farming has very high fixed capital costs in land and machinery, and farmers must invest a lot of labor and resources just to put seeds in the ground. Then they wait months until harvest and sale, during which time their capital is immobile. At harvest, if prices are low, farmers can't hold back their product to bring up prices, or cut back on production to cut costs; they are price takers, not price makers. If they lose money, they must make up their losses the following year, farming their way out of debt by producing more. But increasing production only leads to market saturation, resulting in even lower prices. Most commercial farmers are highly leveraged and only a few crops away from bankruptcy. Of course, farmers try to compensate in many ways by storing grain, selling futures, hedging, leasing more or less land, and cutting back on costs.

But farmers also produce more when prices are high. According to Iowa farm leader George Naylor:

Under the current laissez-faire policy of planting fencerow to fencerow, a farmer is always going to try to produce more bushels to sell – either out of greed or for fear of going broke. If a chemical input can seemingly increase income over cost, they'll use it. But when all farmers follow suit, overproduction results in low prices and our land and water are degraded.[23]

This explains the financial precariousness of commercial farmers – and why the tendency toward overproduction and expansion is especially acute for capitalist agriculture. Subsidies, crop insurance, commodity futures, and export incentives are designed not to support farmers but to maintain the commodity system of capitalist agriculture.[24] These measures – and occasional windfalls like the biofuels boom – just barely help farmers to weather the storms of chronic overproduction and low prices.

The situation is even harder for poor farmers, who typically sell most of their product immediately after harvest because they need money. This is the worst time to sell, because prices are low. Months later, when their meager reserves of food run out, they must buy food on the market – when prices are high. This is when poor farmers go hungry – after they have fed everyone else.

For the last half-century, the stock solutions to this problem has been to intensify production with Green Revolution technologies, credit, and by linking farmers to global markets. But these farmers are poor primarily because they farm very small parcels on marginal agricultural land, not because they don't know how to farm or market their goods. And the global market doesn't help; its low prices are often below their costs of production. Unlike their Northern counterparts, these farmers can't fall back on subsidies. Once smallholders enter into these capitalized forms of production, credit, and marketing, they are exposed to the general trends of overproduction, bankruptcy, and consolidation that characterize capitalist agriculture. This is why the agricultural development scenarios developed by the World Bank quietly admit that their strategies for agricultural development depend on "land mobility," a euphemism that means that most smallholders must leave agriculture to make way for the steady consolidation of agricultural landholdings in fewer and fewer hands.[25]

The never-ending Green Revolution[26]

In the 1960s crop scientist Norman Borlaug was contracted by the Rockefeller and Ford Foundations to develop high-yielding varieties (HYVs) of grain that responded well to high-density planting, irrigation, and high-fertilizer applications. His early successes led Western governments to finance a massive research system, anchored in thirteen international agricultural research centers (IARCs) under a coordinating body called the Consultative Group for International Agricultural Research (CGIAR). Geographically situated in the Vavilov centers of biological diversity, the IARCs collected seeds from the rich pool of cultivars developed by peasant farmers over thousands of years. This genetic material allowed scientists to develop high-yielding hybrid varieties of irrigated wheat, maize, and rice that relied on synthetic fertilizer and pesticides that became the trademark of the Green Revolution.

The Green Revolution was widely celebrated and Borlaug won the Nobel Prize. A closer look calls these accolades into question.

During the heyday of the Green Revolution (1970–90), global per capital food production rose by 11 percent, while the estimated number of hungry people fell by 6 percent. But, in South America, where per capita food supplies rose almost 8 percent, the number of hungry people went up by 19 percent. In South Asia there was a 9 percent increase in food per capita by 1990, but there were also 9 percent more hungry people. (Without China's notable gains, world hunger actually increased by more than 11 percent – from 536 to 597 million.)[27] The Green Revolution experienced its own crisis of overproduction in the 1990s when grain prices crashed and farmers could no longer afford all the seeds and chemicals being offered to them. The number of hungry people exploded to 800 million.[28] Among them were millions of peasant farmers displaced by larger, more capital-efficient farms that had expanded thanks to the Green Revolution.

The social and environmental drawbacks of the Green Revolution were widely documented. These included increased inequality in rural incomes, concentration of land and resources, increasing pest problems, loss of agrobiodiversity, massive farmworker poisonings, salinization, depleted and contaminated aquifers, and the erosion of fragile tropical soils.[29] In both Mexico and India, seminal studies revealed that the Green Revolution's expensive "packages" of HYV seeds and fertilizers favored a minority of economically privileged farmers, put the majority of smallholders at a disadvantage, and led to the concentration of land and resources, increasing rural inequality.[30]

The growth in agricultural production produced some winners and many losers. The winners got all the press. The assumption was that the losers would leave agriculture, move to the cities, and find work in industry. Many did move, but industry was unable to absorb all of the labor. Slums grew exponentially everywhere the Green Revolution was introduced. Others tried to eke out a living in the countryside where both their labor and their products were devalued. Many migrated to the "agricultural frontier," the edges of the forests, and the fragile hillsides, where they cleared new land for farming. All these scenarios drove them deeper into poverty. They went hungry.

Agricultural intensification has been the foundation for every single global campaign to end hunger since the mid-twentieth century – including biotech's new iteration of the Green Revolution: the "Gene Revolution." This time, the campaign calls for GMOs, big data, and precision agriculture. Despite the unending hype surrounding the potential of GMOs to end hunger, a quarter-century after their introduction, GMOs have primarily succeeded in producing feed for livestock and ethanol for automobiles. Poor and hungry people have not been fed by this industry. Behind the unending good news narratives, the Green Revolution creates its own markets, its own science, and its own truths, and, by impoverishing smallholder agriculture, it creates as many hungry people as it saves.[31]

While it is now on the upswing, global economic

growth has been less than 2 percent since the 1980s. This has led to mergers and financial fixes in order to provide expected returns to shareholders. Although capital has concentrated, much of the world is experiencing a recession. However, the poorest "base of the economic pyramid" is growing at 8 percent a year.[32] This growth represents a huge potential market. But what can you sell to people who are too poor to buy smart phones, flat screen TVs, and electric cars? Processed food. What can you sell to 2.5 billion poor farmers? Small packets of seeds, fertilizer, and pesticides. The unstated irony behind the push for a new, genetically engineered Green Revolution is that it responds to the financial needs of corporations, not to the food needs of the poor.

Hidden hunger and the promises of fortification

In 2016 the World Food Prize was awarded to three scientists for their work on crop biofortification.[33] Biofortification genetically engineers food crops like beans, rice, wheat, millet, sweet potatoes, and cassava to contain more zinc, iron, and carotene, ostensibly to address the "hidden hunger" affecting more than 2 billion people worldwide. Hidden hunger can also affect the overweight and obese, and touches all aspects of social and economic life:

> Effects of hidden hunger include child and maternal death, physical disabilities, weakened immune systems, and compromised intellects. Where hidden hunger has taken root, it not only prevents people from surviving and thriving as productive members of society, it also holds countries back in a cycle of poor nutrition, poor health, lost productivity, persistent poverty, and reduced economic growth. This demonstrates why not only the right to food, but also access to the right type of food at the right time, is important for both individual well-being and countries as a whole.[34]

Biofortified varieties are designed to address micronutrient deficiency in remote rural areas by introducing nutrient-enriching genes into the traditional crops that rural people eat, like cassava and sweet potato.[35] Aside from introducing nutrients into rural people's diets, the aim of biofortification is to integrate rural agricultural communities into the global food system. Biofortified crops are a promising way for companies to expand into the seed markets still largely supplied by farmer-to-farmer seed systems. Biofortified staple crops (like root crops and plantains) are more easily accepted than GMOs (maize, soy, or cotton) because they are seen as benefiting the poor. They are a key to opening markets for GMOs in poor countries because, in order to be cultivated, regulations accepting GMOs must be incorporated into the country's seed laws. For this reason, biofortification is often seen as a sophisticated Trojan horse for corporate expansion into food systems still operating outside the commodity system.[36] The big players in the two-decade biofortification push include the Rockefeller Foundation and Syngenta (Golden Rice), Dupont, Monsanto (BioCassva Plus) and the Bill and Melinda Gates Foundation.[37]

But isn't biofortification at least a benign form of genetic engineering? A lab technician working on Golden Rice in the Philippines once assured me: "We don't put bad genes into rice, only good ones!"

The "good genes" of biofortification allow the seed industry to avoid asking why farmers are nutrient-poor after six decades of Green Revolution technologies. It ignores the fact that the spread of the Green Revolution's single-crop monocultures systematically destroyed farm nutrient diversity, and, as a consequence, decimated rural diets. Biofortification's champions invite us to believe that poor nutrition is the natural state of the poor. The remedy is to inject nutrients into the seeds of staple crops – then sell them to farmers.

Nearly 200 years ago, exploited by British capital, Irish peasants were reduced to eating just potatoes – the monoculture of the poor. No amount of bio-fortification would have prevented the potato blight and the "Great Hunger" that killed more than a million people. Hidden hunger under conditions of poverty and exploitation quickly gave way to mass famine. The danger of biofortification is that it misses the causes of nutrient deficiency hiding in plain sight.

The urban version of biofortification – fortified food – adds nutrients to food (rather than crops) to make up for all those that are lost by industrial food processing. In the 1960s the diets of the poor were eroded by the substitution of cheap, processed imports for fresh, local food. Developing countries began adding micronutrients to staple products such as flour, oil, sugar, and margarine, making these products available through antihunger programs. Today, food industry giants like Nestlé, Unilever, PepsiCo, Kellogg, Danone, and General Mills are the ones selling nutrients to the undernourished. To support the trend, in 2005, the World Bank started the Business Alliance for Food Fortification (BAFF). Chaired by Coca-Cola, the partnership includes the major players in the global food industry, like Nestlé, Heinz, Ajinomoto, Danone, and Unilever.[38]

Just as the Green Revolution produced a "science of scarcity" to justify the overproduction of agricultural commodities, so nutritionism has produced the "science of insufficiency" to justify cramming nutrients into staple food crops and food products sold by global monopolies. Nutritionism is a reductionist form of science that avoids addressing the causes of malnutrition and both simplifies and exaggerates the role of nutrients in dietary health.[39] By reducing hidden hunger to a problem of insufficient nutrients – without asking why nutrients are lacking – nutritionism carves out a space for the new, nutrient-enriched products offered by the market.

When hunger is reduced to a problem of micronutrient deficiencies, whoever provides the micronutrients will profit. Addressing the ways the global food system has destroyed traditional sources of nutrients and impoverished people's diets is avoided. Rather than eating a healthy diet made up of diverse, whole, and fresh foods, poor people are sold special, nutrient-enriched, processed food purchased from the food industry. It also allows governments and industry to depoliticize the causes of world hunger and nutrient deficiency by recasting them as technical problems to be solved by technical solutions rather than structural measures like land reform, promotion of agroecological approaches to farming, market reforms, or living wages. Biofortification pioneers and tech-savvy food companies claim that ending hunger is simply about getting the science right. This suggests that hunger has no cause, it just happens – but that science and industry can end it.

People are hungry because they cannot afford to buy food, not because science hasn't figured out what to feed them. Farmers are nutrient-deficient because they no longer grow a balanced diet.

Food waste: the new savior?

There is a lot of concern about food waste, and with good reason. An estimated 30–50 percent of the world's food goes uneaten, worth about US$400 billion a year. That's more than enough to feed the world's hungry. Wasted food means wasted water and energy used in food production, and the needless emission of greenhouse gasses (GHGs) (up to 10 percent of rich nations' emissions). When waste goes to landfills, it produces and releases methane, a powerful GHG that otherwise would have been avoided.[40] In the United States, food provisioning uses up to 10 percent of the total energy budget, 50 percent of national land, and 80 percent of all fresh water. Through food waste, North Americans are throwing away the equivalent of $165 billion in resources each year.[41]

Food waste is not uniform across the globe: 28 percent of global food loss and waste occurs in industrialized Asia, with 23 percent in South and Southeast Asia, 14 percent in North America and Oceania, 14 percent in Europe, 9 percent in sub-Saharan Africa, 7 percent in North Africa and West and Central Africa, and 6 percent in Latin America. While food is wasted on a greater level in post-production in developing countries, food loss occurs on a higher scale in the consumption stages of developed countries.[42]

In farming, production losses are greatest for fresh produce. Produce may not be harvested because of cosmetic imperfections, size, or damage caused by weather, pests, and disease. Sometimes low market prices make it uneconomical to harvest crops. It is difficult for farmers to grow the exact amount that will match market demand, so they grow too much. Each year, 7 percent of planted fields in the United States go unharvested: an estimated US$140 million in crop losses.[43] In the industrial fisheries, up to

60 percent of the catch is discarded before it even reaches port.

No wonder programs are popping up in Europe and North America to "reduce, recycle, and repurpose" food waste as a means to reduce environmental pollution, create jobs, and improve food security. Everything – from composting and energy generation, to food banks and reprocessing – is being thrown at the problem. The US Food Waste Challenge is a private–public initiative between the US government and the agrifoods industry to reduce food waste by 50 percent by 2030 (sound familiar?).[44] Supermarkets are selling "ugly fruit," giving expired products to food banks and selling old produce for animal feed. France recently passed legislation prohibiting grocery stores from throwing away expired food.

The challenge for retail is formidable. Supermarkets regularly stock 50–100 percent more food on their shelves than their customers can possibly buy. Getting them to change is more than simply changing their business model. It implies fundamentally changing the way waste – and food – is viewed.

As food waste goes from being discarded or used up to becoming a commodity, it will become valuable to retailers. So, while there are plenty of good environmental reasons to stop food waste, as retailers recover its value, they will increasingly sell it rather than give it away. When food waste becomes a commodity that the poor must buy, it will cease to address hunger.

Strategies to deal with food waste as a product tend to focus on the effects and not the causes of food waste: overproduction. Waste is endemic to capitalist overproduction. Turning food waste into a commodity or donating it to food banks does nothing to address the cause of waste. People go hungry because they are poor, not because food has gone to waste.

Food: a political commodity

We need to eat every day, but can only eat so much before we are satiated. Dairy, fruits, and vegetables spoil. Grains can be saved for years, but are vulnerable to hoarding, dumping, and financial speculation. Capitalist solutions to overproduction that work for other manufactured commodities (such as planned obsolescence) are more difficult with food. Further, unlike smartphones, cars, or the latest sneakers, food has long been considered to be a human right rather than a privilege. Without food, neither labor, money, nor any of the other commodities have any value. The political and economic centrality of food requires societies to constantly manage production and distribution, whether through the state or the market. For this reason, food and agriculture are almost always in political dispute. Henry Kissinger – the consummate powerbroker – could, at one and the same time, boldly promise an end to hunger, while brazenly stating: "If you control the oil you control the country; if you control food, you control the population."

Ending hunger – or giving that impression – is not a technical problem. It is a political battle with winners and losers. As we'll see, control over how food is produced is at the core of the struggle against hunger.

3

Food, Environment, and Systems Change

More than forty years ago, the book *Limits to Growth* warned that Western civilization was heading for overshoot and collapse. Using computer models, the authors generated optimistic, realistic and pessimistic scenarios to identify resource limits. They established parameters for a discussion on sustainable resource management. The findings were alarming – and controversial. The "realistic" scenarios indicated that humans were using up resources at unsustainable rates. It became clear that extending the developed countries' consumption levels to the developing world could lead to social and environmental collapse.[1]

The Limits to Growth's apocalyptic scenario – and the resource management it counseled – flew in the face of Cold War strategies to knit Third World countries into the capitalist bloc through economic expansion and increased resource use. Accused of being "hysterical," the thesis was swiftly and stridently denounced by a number of prominent scientists. In the ensuing debate, the book became a best-seller. It fueled a budding environmental movement and unleashed a stream of publications regarding global environmental challenges. It is unnerving to revisit *The Limits to Growth* today. The projections were spot on.

Critics have pointed out that the predicted thresholds are constantly being pushed out further into the future. The rate of population growth is leveling off, peak oil has not materialized, and "peak food" continues to be illusory because more land, resources, and technologies are constantly invested in production. But the shifting peaks of resource depletion should not lull us into complacency, nor distract us from the negative impacts of overproduction and unbridled resource use.

As Christian Parenti has pointed out, the most pressing problem with oil is not scarcity, but the fact that there is too much of it and our indiscriminate use of it in the global food system is clogging the earth's atmosphere with greenhouse gases (GHGs).[2] Similarly, the problem with food is not that there isn't enough, but that we produce too much, and the way we do it not only keeps us from ending hunger, it depletes our resource budgets and creates dangerous, and unmanageable, pollution loads. Not only is the environment the destination for the food system's effluvium; also, our bodies are recipients for its toxic levels of salts, sugars, fats, additives, and chemicals. Like the oceans, the aquifers, and the atmosphere, we have become yet another toxic sink for the food system's crap.

Industrial agriculture plays a key role in the "overshoot" of four of nine interconnected planetary boundaries: global warming, biosphere integrity, land degradation, and the nitrogen and phosphorous cycles.[3] A host of "win–win" remedies purports to address these problems by reconciling growth with conservation, profit with mitigation, and extraction with adaptation. But as social ecologist Murray Bookchin pointed out three decades ago:

> To speak of "limits to growth" under a capitalistic market economy is as meaningless as to speak of limits of warfare under a warrior society. The moral pieties that are voiced today by many well-meaning environmentalists are as naive as the moral pieties of multinationals are manipulative. Capitalism can no more be "persuaded" to limit growth than a human being can be "persuaded" to stop breathing.[4]

There are very basic, structural reasons why pro-growth efforts will not solve the food system's environmental problems. By focusing on the effects rather than the systemic causes, some measures will make things worse.

Capitalism, food, and the metabolic rift

Calls to limit the environmental damage caused by the food system are ancient.[5] Historical accounts of forests and soils wasted by agriculture are common, as are those of agricultural expansion and social collapse.[6] Less common are analyses of why agriculture goes through destructive phases, or recognition that some forms of agriculture can actually improve soils and biodiversity, and strengthen environmental resilience.

Capitalism fully emerged in the seventeenth century as a result of the colonization of traditional modes of food production in order to supply cheap food, cheap labor, and cheap raw materials to industry. By privatizing common lands, early capitalism drove a violent geographic transition from the countryside to the cities, impoverishing and dispossessing millions of peasants and creating a massive cheap labor pool for industry. Not all farmers went to the cities; some stayed in the countryside growing subsistence crops and working for wages on the large estates. Because peasant-workers still grew much of their own food, wages paid to them could be kept low. Textile workers subsisted mostly on bread, also made cheap through colonial imports. Rural people provided tremendous food and labor subsidies to industry. This pattern of "functional dualism" in which subsistence agriculture is subjugated to capital-intensive agriculture survives to this day.

Capitalism separated people from nature, defining them as opposing forces in which the role of the former was to conquer the latter. It also created a "metabolic rift" in which urban concentration led to a one-way flow of nutrients from the countryside to the cities where they became waste, polluting rivers, lakes, and oceans. Justus von Leibig, the German chemist who isolated the primary nutrients of plant material, laid the groundwork for the production of synthetic fertilizers. Ironically, the "father of chemical agriculture" argued for recycling nutrients. A "rational agriculture," he claimed, would give "back to the fields the conditions of their fertility." In his *Letters on the Subject of the Utilization of the Municipal Sewage Addressed to the Lord Mayor of London* (1865), von Liebig claimed that pollution of cities with human and animal excrement and the depletion of the natural fertility of the soil were connected. He insisted that organic recycling to return nonsynthetic nutrients to the soil was an indispensable part of a rational agricultural system.[7] Karl Marx, who studied Liebig's work, went a step further, claiming:

> All progress in capitalist agriculture is a progress in the art, not only of robbing the worker, but of robbing the soil; all progress in increasing the fertility of the soil for a given time is a progress toward ruining the more long-lasting sources of that fertility ... Capitalist production, therefore, only develops the techniques and the degree of combination of the social process of production by simultaneously undermining the original sources of all wealth – the soil and the worker.[8]

Early capitalist agriculture addressed declining fertility by digging up graves and old battlefield sites for bones to use as fertilizer. Then new lands were conquered. With the help of slave, convict, and indentured labor, the colonies provided a bounty of food, natural resources, natural fertility, and nitrate-rich guano – all of which were pulled into the metabolic rift – from the wheat fields of the Ukraine to the cane fields of the Americas.

The extermination and exploitation of human beings through genocide, slavery, and indentured servitude opened the colonies to the "primitive accumulation" of land and resources. This new agrarian wealth flowed through industry and finance, bankrolling more military campaigns and imperial expansion. Maize, rice, potatoes, sugar, coffee, and tea were among the staples converted into global commodities, transforming foodscapes around the planet and forming the caloric and financial pillars for what became the colonial food regime. Agricultural commodities were funneled to the imperial centers. From hides for industrial belts to sugar and caffeine to keep starving industrial workers from collapsing, the colonies were forced to supply the empire with the cheap food and resources to fuel the Industrial Revolution. The colonial food regime had arrived.

The global throughput of labor-power and natural resources in the world's food systems dramatically increased pollution loads, while reducing resource budgets worldwide. Booms and busts in global markets steadily drove agriculture to clear more forests and plow up plains, drain swamps, and climb higher up steep hillsides, resulting in soil exhaustion, desertification, and abandonment. From the advancing Sahara and the vanishing

Amazon, to the US Dust Bowl and the loss of the aquifers in the Punjab, capitalism's food regimes have destroyed ecosystems to meet the needs of capital expansion.

Today, the food system's rift between production and consumption not only results in contamination of groundwater, rivers, and oceans, but also to the pollution and degradation of agricultural land itself. As industrial agriculture depletes the soil of its natural fertility, more and more synthetic fertilizers are applied, much more than the plants can use. Only half of the nitrogen applied to maize is absorbed; the rest is lost to runoff, leeching, and volatilization, contributing to nitrification and GHGs. Resource budgets of water and some key nutrients are also in dangerous decline. At current rates, our known reserves of high-grade phosphorous will be depleted by the end of the century.[9]

With the exception of organic farming, capitalist agriculture today is inconceivable without synthetic fertilizer. However, as the hypoxic "dead zone" in the Gulf of Mexico attests, not only has the metabolic rift led to urban and rural pollution, but also capitalist agriculture is now a major source of marine pollution. But pollution is only one of the ways capitalist agriculture is irrational. The wholesale reliance on synthetic fertilizers, pesticides, and herbicides facilitates the spread of monocultures, leading to the loss of agrobiodiversity and resilience, and to the concentration of agricultural land in fewer hands and larger holdings.

The rifts and treadmills of capitalist agriculture

Capitalist agriculture first separated humans from agriculture, then separated animals from plants, severing nutrient cycling between primary and secondary producers and humans.[10] These separations were not driven by capital investment in farming per se, but in the upstream and downstream activities along the food value chain.[11] The lion's share of food's value is captured by the agrifoods industry, either upstream by farm input suppliers (seed, chemical, and farm machinery), or downstream by packers, processors, and retailers. While farmers typically earned 40–50 percent of the food dollar in the 1950s, today they capture less than 20 percent. The power of this agrifoods sector is significant – and constantly growing. In the United States, fewer than 200,000 wholesalers, manufacturers, retailers, and food and beverage companies control the flow of food produced by 3 million farmers for 300 million consumers. Globally, the most powerful of these players are the giant supermarket chains like Walmart, Tesco, and Carrefour.

Despite the plethora of different brands to be found on the supermarket shelf, the food industry is highly concentrated and demands tremendous uniformity from farming. Food commodities are purchased in large, standardized lots. The standardization of food commodities has driven agriculture to concentrate on a half-dozen major grain crops, dominated by a handful of commercial varieties.

The standardization of food depends on single-crop monocultures. This has destroyed the more ecologically sound, complex rotation of crops (such as grains, forage, and legumes), and leaves the soil bare for months out of the year. To cultivate larger and larger areas, newer, bigger farm machinery must be purchased. Anything that simplifies farm management and lowers labor costs – like some GMO crops – will be adopted by farmers because they are on what agricultural economist John Ikerd calls the "technology treadmill":

> These technologies require more capital, but reduce labor and management, allowing each farmer to reduce per unit costs of production while increasing total production. However, as more and more farmers adopt these new technologies, the resulting increases in production cause prices to fall,

eliminating the profits of the early adopters and driving those who refuse to adopt, or adopt too late, out of business. This "technology treadmill" has resulted in chronically recurring overproduction and has been driving farmers off the land for decades.[12]

Integral to the technology treadmill is the "chemical treadmill." Chemical pesticides in agriculture were at first embraced by farmers with the promise of reductions in pest damage, leading to increased profits. Ultimately, the ongoing use of synthetic pesticides and fertilizers increases costs as pests become more chemical-resistant and fertilizers deplete the soil of natural fertility. Secondary pest outbreaks (organisms that weren't formerly major pests but that become so as their natural enemies are destroyed by widespread pesticide use) and soil degradation from overusing fertilizers leave crops more vulnerable to disease. As the continuous use of chemicals produce "superbugs" and "superweeds," farmers are left with little option but to purchase more chemicals each year just to keep on top of weeds and crop damage.

Farmers, farmworkers, and rural residents end up bearing the health risks associated with mechanical production and chemical use (including weed-killers like glyphosate), be they economic, environmental, or health-related, while most of the benefits accrue to off-farm agribusiness corporations. Unlike farmers, the input supply sector receives a return when it sells its product or technology, regardless of whether it works for the farmer or not.

Can't farmers just jump off the treadmill? This is no simple task. Commodity markets buy commodities. Farmers who want to grow something else (or grow differently) must find new suppliers and establish new markets for their goods. Commodities do not exist in isolation; they are part of specific forms of industrial production that not only demand uniformity and volume, but create a particular, low-resilience farming system that is largely devoid of biodiversity. Ecologically, once industrial agriculture has turned the farm-scape into a vast, monocultural desert, it is impossible to cultivate without synthetic fertilizers, pesticides, and herbicides. The environmental effects of this treadmill are catastrophic, as evidenced in four ecological pillars of the food system: soil, water, biodiversity, and climate.

Soil

A third of the world's cultivated land is moderately to highly degraded due to erosion, salinization, compaction, acidification, and chemical pollution. Agriculture is losing about 75 billion tons of crop soil every year – a loss valued at US$400 billion.[13] Soil erosion, degradation, and desertification have reduced agricultural productivity by 50 percent in Africa and 20 percent in Asia. The global loss of soil-based ecosystem services is valued between US$6.3 and $10.6 trillion annually – more than the yearly sales volume of the food industry itself.[14]

Among the drivers of soil degradation, the Food and Agriculture Organization's (FAO) Status of the World's Soil Resources lists farming practices like intensive tillage without adding enough organic matter. This accelerates soil erosion by causing a net loss of soil carbon as CO_2, making soil susceptible to erosion. Nitrous oxide (N_2O), resulting from excessive nitrogen fertilizer use, is also a major contributor to climate change. The report also blames the increase in global meat consumption, and the spread of biofuels as drivers. On the one hand, the FAO assumes these global trends are inevitable. On the other, it suggests that the current model of food production is unsustainable. To solve this dilemma, the FAO proposes systems of "sustainable soil management." But governments have introduced these practices over and over since the 1930s – why do they keep getting abandoned?

Food, Environment, and Systems Change

The answer to this puzzle is in the origins of industrial agriculture and the second global food regime.

After World War II, the huge stockpiles of nitrates used for explosives were converted into cheap fertilizer. Synthetic inputs quickly became the norm that, along with cheap oil, cheap credit, and new farm machinery, fueled the rapid expansion of industrial agriculture. When farms in industrialized countries were no longer able to buy all the fertilizer and farm machinery being produced by the agrichemical industries, the Ford and Rockefeller foundations financed the Green Revolution, a campaign to spread industrial agriculture to the developing world. This opened up markets for the export of surpluses of chemicals, machinery, and new hybrid seed products. The widespread application of nitrogen, phosphorous, and potassium (NPK) to agricultural soils eliminated the practices of cover-cropping, inter-cropping, and relay-cropping with legumes. The substitution of tractors for draft animals also meant that less land was needed to produce legume-based forages. This separated grain cultivation from livestock production, leading to simplified rotations, monocultures, and feedlots. This also eliminated the use of animal manure as a fertilizer and soil conditioner. Agriculture lost its source of organic matter and micronutrients that helped plants resist damage caused by insects and disease.

Pesticide production went from one-tenth of a ton in 1945 to 3 million tons in 1980. Increases in pest damage kept apace. Postwar spikes in fertilizer applications were paralleled by spikes in CO_2, N_2O, and methane emissions. Water and energy use and the rise of ocean acidification all show similar spikes, indicating high resource use and increased pollution as more and more land was brought into industrial production.[15]

The postwar food regime emerged in the wake of two world wars that not only ushered in the standard use of synthetic chemicals and machinery; they also simplified and deskilled agriculture. The enormous grain surpluses in the Global North were exported to the Global South, reversing three centuries of South–North flows established by the colonial food regime. The exports were highly subsidized and rapidly destroyed hundreds of thousands of peasant farms in the South.

Contrary to received wisdom, the intrinsic nature of peasant, indigenous, and smallholder agriculture is not inherently unproductive nor necessarily degrading to soils and the environment. It is true that these farmers have been pushed to marginal, rain-fed lands, and farm smaller and smaller parcels. The resulting soil degradation and decline in yield were only temporarily offset by the introduction of synthetic fertilizers. Today, poor soil and insufficient water – not the genetic vigor of cultivars – are the most limiting factors to production in smallholder agriculture worldwide. This is why soil restoration and conservation are often the first steps in the agroecological restoration of smallholder farms.

Present-day agroecology developed as smallholders struggled to restore their soils and extricate themselves from the Green Revolution's chemical "treadmills" that were driving them bankrupt. With agroecology, farmers use animal manures, compost, legumes, and cover crops to provide nutrients, while increasing organic matter levels, thus helping to maintain soil moisture and protect soil surfaces. Swales, terraces, and alternating contour strips are used to conserve soil and water. Weeds are controlled by cultivating, rotations, cover-cropping, inter-cropping, and mulches. Insect pests are managed by attracting predators with companion planting, interrupting pest cycles and vectors with rotations, alley-cropping, and the use of trap and repellant crops. Management of microclimates, different forms of agroforestry and diversified animal husbandry, along with polycultures and a strong reliance on a rich array of locally adapted land races, are all used in combination to distribute risk and ensure a stable supply of food despite droughts, frosts, and floods. All of this not only restores soil and produces an abundance of food, it also captures carbon and builds climate resilience in our food system.

Soil degradation resulting from agricultural production can occur on large and small, modern or traditional farms. However, soil degradation is not inevitable and conservation practices are well known. The reason these practices are not followed has to do with both the technological packages advanced by the Green Revolution and the market pressures from capitalist food systems to squeeze as much value as possible out of the soil.

The key to restoring soil is the restoration of the agroecosystem. The key to restoring the agroecosystem is working with the world's smallholders – the farmers who produce most of the world's food.

Water

Agricultural runoff not only depletes the soil, but deposits large amounts of nitrogen and phosphorous into rivers, lakes, and oceans that lead to algal blooms. When algae die, their decomposition uses up all the oxygen in the water (hypoxia), resulting in massive fish and crustacean die-off in areas called "dead zones." Since the mid-twentieth century – more or less since the spread of synthetic fertilizers – dead zones around the world have expanded 1000 percent. Today, there are 406 dead zones covering an area larger than the United Kingdom. Prominent dead zones include the Gulf of Mexico (22,729 square kilometers, an area about the size of New Jersey); the Chesapeake Bay (7.25 cubic kilometers), and the Baltic Sea (60,000 square kilometers). In the United States, the rise in industrial meat production is at the root of the problem. The fertilizer runoff from maize and soy plantations (for feed), and the effluent from large, confined animal feedlot operations are to blame for the alarming increase in the size of dead zones.[16] The rise in ocean temperatures is exacerbating the phenomenon.

As climate change increases the frequency and severity of droughts, farmers dig deeper wells in order to water their crops. "Fossil" water – ancient underground sources that can't be recharged by rainfall – are being drained to irrigate crops grown primarily to feed livestock and produce biofuels. From the almond groves of California and the corn fields of Iowa, to the wheat fields of northern India and the North China Plain, agriculture is rapidly depleting these nonrenewable aquifers. Once they are gone, they are gone forever.

Throughout the twentieth century, US agriculture pumped out less than 10 cubic kilometers of water a year. Since 2000, it has been pumping out 25 cubic kilometers per year.[17] India's famous Punjab region – the heartland of the Green Revolution – lost 109 cubic kilometers of water from its Indus River plain aquifer in less than ten years. In northwestern India, the water table is declining at a rate of 30 centimeters per year in an area that covers over 438,000 square kilometers. The primary reason for this groundwater depletion is irrigation for agriculture.[18] (Hydraulic fracturing is adding to water woes. More than one-third of natural gas wells are in regions suffering groundwater depletion.)

Tried and true methods for soil and water conservation are well known. Most have been practiced for centuries:

- maintain high levels of organic matter to absorb and conserve soil moisture;
- constant soil cover to prevent the erosive impact of raindrops and reduce evaporation;
- contour ditches, barriers, bunds, swales, and terraces to stop erosive runoff and conserve water;

- deep-rooting perennial crops and companion planting to hold in soil;
- partial shade (trees, shrubs, and certain crop associations such as the "Three Sisters" combination of maize, beans, and squash)

For decades, these forms of agroecological management have built farm resilience for smallholders around the world. In Central America and in Cuba, this resilience was measured following catastrophic hurricanes. Farmers in the Campesino a Campesino (farmer to farmer) movement for sustainable agriculture were found to have less crop damage, less erosion, and fewer landslides and gullies than their conventional neighbors. They were able to resist the impact of the storm and bounce back faster in its aftermath.[19] The superior resilience of agroecologically managed systems has been demonstrated time and again.[20] Agroecology's whole system approach to climate resilience goes far beyond "drought-tolerant" seeds that are useless in the face of hurricanes. Unlike the one-gene, one-trait, one-crop approach adopted by industry, agroecology builds diversified, structural resilience into the whole farming system to help farmers cope with floods, droughts, heat waves, cold snaps, pest outbreaks, and even market volatility.

Unfortunately, almost all these methods run counter to the dominant model of industrial agriculture. The corporate fanfare surrounding the potential of "drought-tolerant" and "climate-smart" GM seeds to cope with climate change focuses only on the cultivar, rather than on the farm system as a whole. The silence regarding the systemic methods of dealing with the wide range of climate-related severe weather is a reflection of the fact that climate-smart seeds are themselves commodities marketed by agribusiness monopolies, while agroecological methods are freely shared knowledge.

The spread of industrial agriculture has not only displaced tried and true soil and water conservation practices, it has depleted and contaminated the world's agricultural water supplies, leaving entire regions vulnerable to drought. The "climate-smart" seeds promoted by industry and conventional agricultural science are not only insufficient to address the systemic vulnerability of industrial agriculture to drought, but, by avoiding the question of why water is a problem, they also ignore the structural drivers of water scarcity.

Biodiversity

Due to the massive amounts of carbon emissions, a sixth mass planetary extinction will move from the realm of possibility to probability by 2100. It is not a question of *if* the next extinction will happen, but *when* – sometime over the next 10,000 years. The tipping point is the amount of carbon absorbed by oceans, about 310 Gigatons. This happens to be the estimated amount of carbon that human activities will have added to the atmosphere by the year 2100.

This scenario is terrifying. However, extinctions due to intensive agricultural production have already taken place and are continuing. While the steadily disappearing numbers of charismatic mega fauna (including whales, elephants, lions, rhinos, gorillas, etc.) are widely lamented, the "Great Insect Die-Off" is an indication that we are traveling the road to mass extinction faster than we realize.

In the past four centuries, 130,000 species of invertebrates have disappeared, primarily due to habitat loss. But more recently, extinctions increased at an unprecedented rate. In Germany, studies carried out on nature reserves surrounded by agricultural areas show a 75 percent decline in flying insects since 1990. The analysis suggests that agricultural pesticides are the cause.[21] Insects are the "canaries in the mineshaft." Because of their position in the food chain, the massive insect die-off will have a negative tropic cascading effect on birds, fish, and mammals.

Over 70 percent of the world's agrobiodiversity has already been lost since the introduction of the Green Revolution. Not only has the *in situ* diversity been lost – in which seeds are developed, saved, and planted by farmers over millennia – displaced by just five commodity crops, each with just a handful of varieties, but the knowledge of how to grow these varieties and associate them in cropping mixtures for maximum resilience and productivity is also being lost.

With the transition to hybrid varieties, heirlooms seeds are stored *ex situ* at the centers for international agricultural research and the Svalbard Global Seed Vault in Norway. This stopgap conservation measure does not address the causes behind the loss of seed diversity. Further, *ex situ* seeds do not adapt to changing environmental conditions as do *in situ* seeds. Over centuries, traditional farmers developed seeds in diversified farming systems, in the centers of crop origins (Vavilov centers of genetic diversity). To this day, the wild relatives of domesticated crops in the centers of origin are sources for genetic resilience.

Many farmers continue growing traditional landraces and conserving their wild relatives, without any government support. This *in situ* conservation of seeds not only maintains a dynamic, living genetic pool of agrobiodiversity that is constantly adapting to climate change, it also decentralizes and democratizes control over the world's genetic heritage. If we want to conserve seeds, we need to conserve the farmers who are keeping them viable.

The loss of agrobiodiversity, while acknowledged by proponents of the Green Revolution, is treated only as a problem of losing the genetic diversity of seeds – thus *ex situ* seed banks are proposed as a solution. But the loss of on-farm cultivar diversity reflects an even larger loss of wild relatives, wildlands, and habitat diversity that is the basis for the species diversity of insects, invertebrates, birds, and other animal species. Agriculture's role in mass extinction is more influential than is largely acknowledged.

Climate change

The classical political economists who studied agriculture and capitalism couldn't have predicted the most irreversible consequence of the metabolic rift: global warming. Industrial crop production is directly responsible for over 14 percent of global

GHGs.[22] One reason for this is that 50 percent of all applied fertilizer ends up in the atmosphere or in local waterways. Livestock alone produces 18 percent of GHGs.[23] Deforestation, much of which is undertaken to make way for agriculture, constitutes another 18 percent of global emissions.[24] As Annie Shattuck points out, "What we eat is responsible for more carbon pollution than all the world's planes, trains, and automobiles. Between the forests and fields converted to agriculture and pollution directly from farming, what we eat accounts for nearly a third of all the gases contributing to climate change."[25]

Land clearing for agriculture is a major contributor to GHGs. Conventional environmental wisdom blames peasant farmers for the 1.7–2.4 Gigatons of carbon emitted yearly due to deforestation. It is true that during the latter half of the twentieth century peasant farmers engaged in substantial land clearing in places like the Amazon and the Central American rainforest. But they were often part of a larger agrarian transition in which industrial agriculture pushed peasants out of prime agricultural areas. To avoid the issue of land reform, government "colonization" programs encouraged poor farmers to migrate to the "agricultural frontier" where they felled tropical forests with slash-and-burn agriculture. Large cattle ranchers followed close behind, pushing the peasants deeper into the forest.[26]

According to one global estimate, over 70 percent of deforestation results from growing commercial crops.[27] The bulk of GHG emissions resulting from land use change is driven by gigantic plantations of soy, maize, sugar cane, and palm oil. Small farmers displaced by these plantations must clear new land, thus increasing carbon emissions even more. In sub-Saharan Africa, displaced farmers encroach on the rangeland of pastoralists, weakening the resilience and livelihoods of both. The tragic irony of this model of food production is that 24 percent goes to waste, 35 percent goes to animal feed, and 3 percent goes to biofuels.

But, as we have seen, not all agriculture systems are created equal. While industrial agriculture represents the majority of emissions from global agriculture, agroecological practices – used primarily by small-scale farmers – not only contribute fewer emissions, but also sequester more carbon and other GHGs. No matter, when the figures for agriculture's negative impact on the ecology of the planet are calculated, all forms of agriculture are thrown into the same, industrial sack.

The blatant conflation of different production systems not only ignores the benefits of approaches like agroecology and agroforestry, it hides the destructive dynamics of the grain–oilseed–livestock complex and invites us to believe that measures like "sustainable intensification" and "land-sparing" implemented on vast soy and maize plantations are actually offsetting the increased emissions resulting from the spread of feed and fuel crops. Further, it ignores how grains and oilseed grown for feed (no matter how "sustainable" the methods), support the growth of an industry whose breeding sites, factory farms, feedlots, slaughter houses, and packing plants demand enormous amounts of energy and emit high levels of CO_2, methane, and airborne contaminants, and how they deplete and pollute rivers, streams, and aquifers. The "food miles" of these operations also contribute to GHGs, as grains grown on one continent are shipped long distances overseas to feeder operations, that then ship young animals across borders to be fattened, then somewhere else to be slaughtered, all before being exported as meat. As long as we focus on technical fixes, rather than on whole systems, we will be underestimating the ecological damage being done by the interlocking sectors.

The high contribution to GHGs from industrial agriculture stems not only from the overuse of chemicals and its dependence on fossil fuels, but also from the loss of forests, vegetation, and soil organic matter inherent to production practices, and the tendency of large, industrial farms to displace smaller, more diverse farming systems. Nearly 40 percent of industrial production does not produce food for people, but for feed and fuel crops, both high carbon-emitting sectors. Industrial agriculture's practices need changing, but so does the larger, interlocked, global form of production. A linchpin in capitalism's form of production is industrial livestock.

The ecological hoofprint

The food system's environmental failings with soil, water, biodiversity, and climate change are nowhere as evident as with the rise of the industrial grain–oilseed–livestock complex.

Meat's "ecological hoofprint" uses up 30 percent of all agricultural land in a pattern that geographer Tony Weis refers to as "oceans" of monocultures and "islands" of concentrated animals.[28] Great volumes of maize, soy, barley, sorghum, oats, and canola are grown on vast plantations to be processed into feed for industrial livestock. Capital-intensive CAFOs (confined animal feedlot operations) concentrate millions of pigs, poultry, and cattle in cramped pens and corrals, where high-protein feed is fed to fast-growing, high-producing animals that are pumped with antibiotics and hormones to encourage high productivity and fast growth. Not limited to industrial countries, this highly polluting form of production is spreading worldwide.

> [This is] steadily displacing agro-pastoral systems in which farm animals' multifunctional use-value (energy, manure, hides, wool, etc.,) are being replace by the exchange value of their flesh, eggs and milk ... This transformation is bound to a singular organizing imperative: to accelerate the turnover time of production, or increase rates of weight gain, laying and lactation.[29]

"Biological speed-up" is the holy grail of capitalist agriculture because it produces more relative value in a given amount of time. Selective breeding, genetic engineering, and the use of antibiotics and growth hormones drastically reduce the growing time of animals on factory farms and intensify the lactations of short-lived dairy cows.[30] The negative consequences of biological speed-up are well documented. Broiler chickens "mature" in just eight weeks, growing over a pound a week while sitting in the dark on manure-caked floors because so much of the energy they consume is converted into growth that they can't stand up. Dairy cows are biologically exhausted after three lactations and sold for hamburger meat. The CAFO manure ponds are major environmental hazards and the hormones and antibiotics used in animal production disrupt human hormonal development and endocrine functions, as well as creating resistant bacterial strains.

Biological speed-up also determines what kind of meat dominates world markets. The spectacular growth of poultry and hogs (compared to cattle) explains why they now make up 70 percent of the meat eaten in the world. This drives what Weis calls the "meatification" of world diets: "Seventy billion farm animals are slaughtered, yearly – up from just 7 billion 60 years ago. Projections indicate that by 2050, 120 billion animals a year will be slaughtered, a fifteen-fold increase in less than a century."[31]

Nowhere in the panoply of industrial agriculture's climate-smart toolbox is there any alternative to the meat industry – the largest, most polluting, unhealthy, carbon-spewing sector in agriculture. All other sectors are exhorted to conserve soil, water, and biodiversity in order to mitigate and adapt to the environmental devastation wreaked by the grain–oilseed–livestock complex. The expansion of grain and soy-fed meat is assumed to be an inevitable consequence of capitalist development. If this is true, then it is capitalist development that must be questioned.

Technical change versus systems change: from green revolutions to gene revolutions

The losses of soil, water, and biodiversity, together with the steady advance of climate change, have brought forth a flurry of responses from the very industries whose forms of production and consumption are at the heart of global ecological overshoot. These responses are characterized by a preference for technical fixes to immediate problems rather than systemic solutions to address the roots of the problems.

Technical fixes are designed to stabilize the existing food regime – not change it. This is why they frequently come into conflict with more systemic approaches (like land reform and market reforms). The basic criteria for a regime-friendly technical fix is that it be patentable, profitable, compatible with the existing technological model, and not challenge the social relations of production or large, industrial economies of scale. Preferably, it only temporarily addresses the problem, leaving room for future innovations. In other words, technical fixes are preferred when they can be turned into commodities.

For example, in the 1990s, when the multiple crises of overproduction, growing rural poverty, and ecological damage nearly ground the Green Revolution to a halt, many prominent experts working in agricultural development called for a post-Green Revolution transition to sustainable agriculture. Gordon Conway, a prominent agricultural ecologist, invited researchers and farmers to work together in a "doubly green" revolution to raise production and conserve natural resources by finding alternatives to the Green Revolution's chemical approach.[37]

Under new management from the World Bank, the Consultative Group for International Agricultural Research (CGIAR) announced a "[thrice] green revolution: green for productivity; green for environmental sustainability; and green for increased income as the entry point to improved living conditions, dealing with the access side of food security." Ismail Serageldin, CGIAR's new, bank-appointed chairman, claimed: "We are committed to the new paradigm of development in which cutting-edge science can be combined with traditional knowledge; in which community-based action is recognized as essential for effectiveness; and in which empowerment of farm families, and primarily of women, is paramount."[33] A CGIAR–NGO (nongovernmental organization) committee was formed with agroecologist pioneer Miguel Altieri as chair. The committee immediately began producing research and reports, as well as sponsored conferences, village-level agroecology workshops, and farmer-to-farmer exchanges. It seemed the Green Revolution was on the verge of change.

Change came, but in the form of biotechnology.

The World Bank's downsizing and restructuring of the CGIAR opened the Green Revolution to private financing and genetic engineering. As the resources for GMOs grew, support for agroecology and the CGIAR–NGO committee shrank. The committee was eventually abandoned. The Bill and Melinda Gates Foundation replaced the Rockefeller Foundation as the philanthropic flagship of the Green Revolution, reflecting the ascendance of the free market over publicly funded research. Genetically modified crops led the charge of the new "Gene Revolution."

Chemical companies like Monsanto and Syngenta inserted glyphosate-resistant genes into the existing high-yielding varieties (HYVs) developed by the Green Revolution. This allowed farmers to spray herbicide on their fields, killing the weeds instead of the crops. Genes from *Bacillus thuringiensis* (Bt) – which had been a homemade organic pesticide farmers dusted on crops selectively – were genetically inserted into existing maize varieties, making the entire corn plant toxic to pests. Disregarding the warnings from ecologists, entomologists, and weed scientists that glyphosate-resistant and Bt crops would quickly produce superweeds and superbugs (they did), the Gene Revolution steadily reset the agricultural development agenda. The CGIAR began focusing on genetic engineering for bio-fortified and drought-resistant crops.

Fifteen years later, when the Gene Revolution transition was complete (and the world's hungry had grown from 750 million to over a billion), Gordon Conway produced a second iteration of *The Doubly Green Revolution* called *One Billion Hungry: Can We Feed the World?* This time he argued for accepting agroecological techniques alongside GMOs. The problem of hunger was so bad, we needed "all solutions."[34] While Conway glossed over fifteen years of agrarian capitalism in which monopolies and the free market ignored agroecology and systematically ravaged smallholder agriculture, *One Billion Hungry* made it clear that, after a brief moment of interest, the Green Revolution had abandoned agrocecology's systems approach for the quick-fix commodities offered by industry.[35]

Agroecological methods were not thrown out *in toto*, but they were adopted only to the extent they were compatible with GMOs and didn't require any capital investment. The approach was dubbed "sustainable intensification." It nested within the new industrial rubric of "climate-smart" agriculture.

The trifecta of climate-smart agriculture

The notion that farming more intensively can produce more food on less land is not new. In the eighteenth century, English High Farming intensified production with imported guano as it displaced peasant farmland. The Green Revolution increased productivity on the world's best agricultural soils and claimed to have avoided agricultural expansion onto new lands.

But the claim that intensifying agriculture can not only produce more on less land, but also pollute less while using fewer resources, conserve biodiversity, and be resilient in the face of climate change is unique to the framework of climate-smart agriculture. The core strategy is sustainable intensification, and its Holy Grail is land sparing. The brief, working definitions of the three, interrelated concepts are as follows:

- climate-smart agriculture: a trifecta (win–win–win) framework to increase productivity while simultaneously strengthening resilience and reducing greenhouse gas emissions;
- sustainable intensification: techniques to produce more food on less land without increasing pollution;
- land sparing: conserving biodiversity by avoiding agricultural expansion into natural habitats.

These concepts allow for a wide range of production techniques. Scale, levels of capitalization and mechanization, and the specific nature of techniques per se are irrelevant. Everything from peasant agroecology to CAFOs are permitted, as long as the specific technique or innovation is an improvement over the prior practice. These techniques are part of a global climate adaptation strategy that must not only improve upon existing practices, but must also integrate all food production into global value chains.

At their core, the concepts share the same basic claims and assumptions regarding hunger, climate, biodiversity, and agriculture. The overarching justification for the climate-smart trifecta is, of course, that to end hunger we must increase the production of food (read: we must continue the overproduction of food). We have already dispensed with this myth, but without it, support for the trifecta falls apart. Unsurprisingly, it is the basis for all the corollary claims and assumptions.

The first assumption is that chemical-intensive monocultures are more productive than ecological-intensive polycultures. This grounds the claim that only the application of synthetic fertilizers, pesticides, herbicides, and GM seeds can produce enough food to feed the world.

The second assumption is that agriculture necessarily destroys biodiversity. This grounds the claim that limiting the destruction of biodiversity to intensively farmed, chemically dependent monocultures will avoid agricultural expansion onto new land, thus conserving biodiversity and avoiding an increase in GHG emissions.

The third assumption is that inefficient application of chemical inputs – not the rates of application – is the cause of agricultural pollution and GHGs. The gains to efficiency (through precision agriculture) will bring higher profit margins to farmers and they will have no need to expand operations onto new lands.

The genius of these assumptions is that they are designed to reboot the Green Revolution approach to agriculture, while steering us away from any assessment of how the larger corporate food regime (in which the Green Revolution is embedded) undermines climate-smart goals of resilience, productivity, and reduced GHG emissions. These assumptions are deeply flawed.

The widely held assumption that the Green Revolution's large-scale, chemical-intensive monocultures are more productive than smallholder polycultures is not borne out on the ground. It is true that large, industrial monocultures produce more per unit of labor because of their high degree of mechanization. It is also true that a hectare planted to monocultural maize will produce more maize than a hectare planted to the traditional maize–beans–squash polyculture. But the net primary productivity per hectare (the net amount of biomass produced by plants) of polycultures is consistently higher than that of monocultures. Small farms also consistently out-produce large farms in pounds per acre.[36] Under certain conditions and crop mixes, polycultures can "over-yield," producing more per plant when grown in crop associations than in monocultures.[37] There is ample evidence demonstrating the high productivity per unit of land and the strong resilience of agroecologically managed peasant agriculture, as well.[38]

Industrial agriculture destroys biodiversity. The Green Revolution's fungicides and herbicides sterilize the soil biota; pesticides annihilate insect and bird populations, and monocultures replace hundreds of plant species with just one cultivar. This explains the two-decade effort by the CGIAR to mediate the Green Revolution's environmental externalities.

The land-sparing environmental argument is loosely based on the theory of "Island Biogeography" developed by E.O. Wilson and Robert MacArthur.[39] Island biogeography originally modeled the rates of species colonization and extinction on islands in the ocean. The bigger and closer the islands were to the mainland, the greater the biodiversity (numbers and kinds of birds and plants). Conservation biologists applied the theory to forest biodiversity. They treated the forest as a species-rich "mainland" and the neighboring agricultural fields as an inert "ocean" they called a matrix. The bigger and closer that forest fragments in the agricultural matrix were to the main forest "mainland," the richer they would be in biodiversity. The agricultural matrix was also assumed to be devoid of species and biodiversity.

However, while this theory may hold for industrial

agriculture, it does not describe the extensive patch-works of small, diversified, agroecological farms. In their book *Nature's Matrix*, researchers John Vandermeer, Ivette Perfecto, and Angus Wright quantitatively demonstrated that agroecological farms are rich in biodiversity and actually serve to replenish and enrich biodiversity in the surrounding forests.[40]

To the end of his days, Norman Borlaug, the father of the Green Revolution, held that high-producing, early adopters of HYVs would push less efficient, late adopters out of business, thus reducing the total amount of farmland. This turned out to be false. Global studies show an increase of both agricultural yields and cultivated areas. This is due in part to the fact that instead of being pushed out of agriculture, many peasant farmers where pushed to the agricultural frontiers. It is also due to the "Jevons paradox" in which, as prices fall due to increased or more efficient production, demand expands, which brings more land into production.[41]

Writing in her blog for the journal *Nature*, professor Claire Kremen points to the example of Peru:

Where the government encouraged investment in oil palm agriculture, researchers found that highly-capitalized, intensive growers used less land than small to mid-sized producers that had lower-yielding operations. However, this example of land-sparing did not lead to nature-sparing, since the highly-capitalized growers disproportionately cleared primary forest sites for their operations.[42]

George Naylor, a grain farmer from Iowa explains the US's dilemma:

> The Golden Fact/Big Lie . . . claims that by increasing yields on existing farmland, we can avoid the need to convert virgin land – like the rainforest, marshland, or the savanna – to commodity production. The opposite is actually true; any time you increase yields, you cut the cost of production, making cultivation on marginal land even more likely.[43]

The lack of a systems framework inherent in climate-smart agriculture, sustainable intensification, and land sparing lead to categorical errors regarding the true extent of GHG emissions. In his review of the World Bank's climate-smart evaluation of Argentina's conversion of the pampas into "vast monocultures of no-till soy, maize, and wheat," Marcus Taylor of Queens University in Canada writes:

> [Judging] "smartness" in terms of the relative change between previous and present methods,

the Bank lauds chemical-intensive monocropping as an exemplary technology on the basis that it represents an improvement over the even-more ecologically inefficient form of industrial agriculture that immediately preceded it . . . Argentine soy production underscores the factory production of livestock, including massive industrial pig farms in the US and China. Such industrial meat production is (1) rampantly inefficient in terms of nutrient use; (2) a major contributor to climate change; and (3) has incredibly poor local environmental impacts. As such, "climate-smart agriculture" in Argentina stands as the foundation for "climate-stupid consumption."[44]

Climate-smart agriculture and sustainable intensification do not address the mode of agricultural production (capitalism), the inequitable distribution of the means of production (land, labor, capital), or the unequal distribution of income and wealth that leaves people unable to purchase sufficient amounts of healthy food. Rather, they call for technological changes with industrial forms of production compatible with the existing politics and structures of the corporate food regime. The underlying premise is that new agricultural technologies are either sufficient to solve the problem of hunger and environmental degradation, or will eventually drive new innovations, or are the best we can hope to accomplish within capitalist agriculture at this time.

By putting capitalism itself safely outside its purview, these approaches not only affirm and normalize capitalist agriculture, they also avoid addressing how capital favors some forms of production over others and ignores how some forms can exploit others. For example, large-scale plantation agriculture for feed and fuel crops crowds out food-growing smallholders without providing jobs to compensate for the loss of livelihoods. Contract farming traps farmers in a serf-like form of debt bondage, no matter how sustainable the intensification. Large-scale monocultures and CAFOs, with all their inherent ecological and economic risk, fit nicely within the climate-smart/sustainable intensification framework: all they have to do is reduce the footprint of their manure ponds and be more efficient with the tremendous quantities of chemicals, hormones, antibiotics, water, and energy they consume. The quality of the food (or of the diets of consumers) is not of concern, nor is the power of the monopolies invested in continuing this form of production.

But wouldn't it be better if all farms produced more food on less land and were more sustainable? Well, perhaps. But do we want to sustain CAFOs, contract farming, and monocultures on plantations or huge farms? Shouldn't we be looking at the small-scale agroecological farms that are already producing high yields using practices that work in concert with the environment and restructure the food system to ensure their economic future?

Land to finance it all: the next agrarian transition

Driven by the need for agrifoods corporations to expand, the food system is embarking on an unprecedented transition. The old, clunky techniques of gene transfer are being superseded by much quicker forms of direct DNA manipulation and nanotechnologies. "Digital agriculture" will collect massive amounts of geographic and agronomic data and use satellite information systems to direct new, sophisticated farm machinery in the application of synthetic fertilizers and pesticides in the latest iteration of "precision agriculture." All the major food and agricultural monopolies, from Monsanto-Bayer, John Deere, Cargill, Nestlé, Walmart, and Amazon, will use these big data systems. As these giants merge among themselves, the entire food value chain will go through another round of consolidation.

And where will farmers get the money to buy the new machinery and pay for the new services? From land. Thanks to the commodities boom and the relaxing of financial regulations, farmland is changing hands and undergoing a period of rising financialization. On the one hand, farmers are taking out new mortgages and even selling land and leasing it back in order to raise the cash that will keep them ahead of the new technology treadmill; on the other, land is simply being grabbed from farmers that are too poor to resist the power of corporations.

Land is not just being consolidated into bigger parcels; the ownership of farmland is passing from farmers to the financial sector. Mortgages are chopped up and repackaged, then sold – again and again. Millions of bits of farmland value are traded every second in global financial markets. This has created a speculative bubble in farmland value that has placed agricultural land out of reach of the poor, as well as young and beginning farmers.

The knitting together of food production, farmland value, and speculative global financial capital is a process Madeline Fairbairn of the University of California calls "gold with yield."[45] Following the 2008–11 food price spikes, both food commodities and land increased in value, unleashing a land rush. Between 2000 and 2016, agribusiness investors "grabbed" more than 24 million hectares of land from smallholders and pastoralists around the world.[46] Oxfam estimates that the combined land grabbed for agriculture, extractive industries, and pure speculation is more than 81 million acres – an area the size of Portugal.[47]

This is not good news for farmers, the food system, or the environment. Aside from the destruction of industrial agriculture, the time horizon of a speculator is minutes – or even seconds. The time horizon for an ecological farmer, concerned about the soil, the aquifer, and biodiversity, is generations. Land stewards, not speculators, will make agriculture sustainable.

A call for action: who is listening?

In 2017, more than 15,000 scientists from 184 countries signed an impassioned letter to world leaders, claiming that "humanity is not taking the urgent steps needed to safeguard our imperiled biosphere." They listed environmental damages over the last twenty-five years that are driving our planet past a number of tipping points:

- the amount of fresh water available per head of population worldwide has reduced by 26 percent;
- the number of ocean "dead zones" – places where little can live because of pollution and oxygen starvation – has increased by 75 percent;
- nearly 300 million acres of forest have been lost, mostly to make way for agricultural land;
- global carbon emissions and average temperatures have shown continued significant increases;
- human population has risen by 35 percent;
- collectively the number of mammals, reptiles, amphibians, birds, and fish in the world has fallen by 29 percent.[48]

This was actually the second call, following the "World Scientists' Warning to Humanity" in 1992. Then, 1,500 scientists signed a letter penned by the Union of Concerned Scientists that "[called] on humankind to curtail environmental destruction and cautioned that a great change in our stewardship of the Earth and the life on it is required, if vast human misery is to be avoided ... Fundamental changes were urgently needed to avoid the consequences our present course would bring."

Instead, capitalism entered into a phase of neoliberal globalization in which environmental and market regulations were abandoned in favor of what was euphemistically called the "free market." Neoliberal capitalism opened the world's resources and the global food system to the highest bidder, sending the world in the opposite direction from the course called for by the world's leading scientists. That a second letter pleads the same case a quarter of a century later is more than a worrisome reflection of the deafness of world leaders. It is an indictment against a political-economic system that, despite its unprecedented wealth, is unable to end poverty and hunger, and despite its formidable corporate power, is unable to control economic growth. Overshoot of the earth's human carrying capacity is driven by capitalism.

4

Who *Can* Feed the World Without Destroying It?

The corporate food regime is not ending hunger or ensuring dietary health for the world's people. Nor is it effectively addressing the problems of climate change, environmental destruction, or resource depletion. As the global economy becomes increasingly inequitable, good food and clean, healthy environments have become entitlements for the privileged, rather than universal rights for all. In the wake of the social and environmental breakdown of how we produce, distribute, and consume our food, many people are calling for reforms to fix a broken global food system.

This assumes that the food system once worked well. The thinking is that with the right technology and fair global markets, with safety nets for food security, and with the participation of women and underprivileged communities, we'll fix the food system. While all those things are needed, the question is, when did the food system work well? If we "fix" it, what are we returning to?

The global food system is a slow-moving disaster, but it is not broken. It is working precisely as a capitalist food system is supposed to work: it expands constantly, concentrating wealth in a few, powerful monopolies, while transferring all the social and environmental costs onto society. These costs are borne inequitably by women, the poor, indigenous peoples, people of color, the working class, rural communities – the most exploited and vulnerable. The exploitation of people and resources for the accumulation of wealth leads to periodic crises of overproduction. These are resolved by destroying the existing wealth, forms of production, and the markets of weaker economies and communities in order to build new ones, thus reinitiating another round of accumulation. Austrian economist Joseph Schumpeter called this "creative destruction" and lauded it as part of capitalism's entrepreneurial motor of progress.[1]

This model "worked" as long as capitalism was expanding and had the possibility to exploit new lands and new, cheap pools of labor. Technological innovation and entrepreneurship delivered an ever greater supply of food. But new resources now cost more to find and existing resources are being polluted. As the world's population levels off, market expansion will cease to be a remedy for the cyclical crises of overaccumulation. Capitalism is entering a late period in which wealth is accumulated by being financially squeezed out of the value created through production. Food itself has become a means for financial speculation.

The problem for the capitalist food system is not overpopulation, but the specter of stagnant population growth and of communities too poor to buy the food being produced. The problem for the world's population is not food scarcity, but the food system that supplies it. Creative destruction in a finite world was always a dangerous proposition. Today's global food system is "creatively destroying" the ability of the earth to support human life. A food system that depends on unlimited growth, exploitation, periodic financial crises, and that is running out of resources, can't be "fixed": it must be transformed.

At the height of the food price crisis, the four-year International Assessment of Agriculture Knowledge, Science and Technology for Development (IAASTD) warned: "The way the world grows its food will have to change radically to better serve the poor and hungry if the world is to cope with growing population and climate change while avoiding social breakdown and environmental collapse."[2]

This is not a call for minor adjustments. It implies a thorough transformation of our laws, regulations, trade regimes, multilateral institutions – and our forms of government. It means that we can't end hunger or environmental destruction without changing the political-economic system in which the food system is embedded.

The urgency and scope of this proposition causes a lot of angst among experts and world leaders: how do we use our existing institutions to transform those same institutions? To remain in power, politicians must convince the governed that they will deliver progress. Since the dawn of capitalism, the motor for progress has been economic growth – no matter what the social and environmental costs amount to. No one gets elected by promising less growth. Now growth itself is the problem. We can no longer consume our way out of global crises.

For the food system, this predicament is addressed by offering up a relentless mix of new products liberally seasoned with hubris, blind hope, and shallow optimism – even if claims of progress contradict what is actually happening on the ground.[3] It is bad enough to be incessantly flogged by technological fixes that lead us farther and farther away from the causes of hunger and environmental destruction. But when governments and multilateral organizations misrepresent the hard facts of hunger, and when the mantra of "doubling food production" is constantly repeated by experts who know better, the result is a cynical body politic. Wall Street may be on the upswing, but confidence in social institutions is at an all-time low.

If the capitalist food system can't feed the world without destroying it, who can?

This is where green techno-fixes and participatory alternatives are usually inserted into the discussion: organic farming, grass-fed beef, permaculture, farmers' markets, community-supported agriculture, urban farming, food waste recovery, even agroecology. Despite their documented successes on the ground, these proposals are routinely swatted to the sidelines, where they are either ignored or unproblematically subsumed as complimentary add-ons to the existing food regime. The rationale runs something like this: the alternative is not as productive as the existing system, it is too labor-intensive, or it can't be scaled up. But because the problems of hunger and environmental destruction are so overwhelming, let's add them to the basket of responses, because we need all the solutions we can get.

Being added to the big tent of solutions is arguably better than being ignored. A perusal of the Food and Agriculture Organization (FAO), Consultative Group for International Agricultural Research (CGIAR), and corporate agrifoods websites reveals a dizzy mix of genetically modified organisms (GMOs), land sparing, climate-smart and precision agriculture, agroecology, agroforestry, conservation agriculture, and a host of promising people-friendly technologies. The retail sector, dependent as it is on plastic packaging, long-distance food miles, monocultures, and the grain–oilseed–livestock complex, populates its websites with the good news of organic products, their own "farmers" markets, and food waste and community food aid programs. The suggestion is that all these solutions are happily working together for a better food system. But the "all solutions" approach obscures tremendous contradictions.

The international agricultural research center (IARC) budgets are hopelessly skewed toward industrial agriculture and GMOs. The amount of money available to small farmers, women, and farmers of color in the US Farm Bill is insignificant when compared to the size of commodity programs and food aid entitlements. As Andy Fisher points out in his analysis of the "unholy alliance" between corporate America and antihunger groups, the emergency food system has become an industry. The "hunger industrial complex" coopts antihunger efforts, directing them away from addressing economic inequality and wages so low that workers must rely on public aid to survive, and away from low prices paid to farmers and offshore product sourcing. The problem is not hunger but poverty. The solution is not charity but an increase in the political power of the poor.[4]

The contradictions and imbalances of political and economic power between these different proposals in the all solutions approach are swept under the rug. The difficulty in incrementally changing the existing food regime by dint of promising alternatives is that none of the proposals in and of themselves can compete with the market power, institutional support, and political backing enjoyed by the industrial food system. Without a concerted strategy to transform the structures of the food system, these alternatives will remain just that: marginal alternatives.

But how do we change the rules and regulations when the very notion of regulation has been abandoned for free market capitalism? How do we create the political will for change when governments themselves are an integral part of neoliberal capitalism? How do we build social power when the public sphere has been decimated by thirty years of privatization? What vision will guide us out of the technocratic, free market dystopia that has captured our food system?

The counter-movements

In his exhaustive studies of capitalism, economist Karl Polanyi discovered that the system always alternated between periods of liberalization and periods of reform. During liberalization, markets were deregulated and tremendous wealth was concentrated. Society at large suffered as free markets privatized public goods and destroyed social institutions, devastating communities, livelihoods, and the environment. Then, the inevitable crisis of capital accumulation would bring about a financial crash and economic ruin.

In the midst of crisis, people rose up in what Polanyi called a "counter-movement," forming cross-class alliances and demanding radical change. The strength of these social movements empowered reformists to implement reforms.[5] The last global example of this was the Great Depression that followed the Roaring Twenties and the stock market crash of 1929. Millions of workers and the unemployed took to the streets and organized unions and political parties. Capitalism's grip on society was slipping. Terrified that people were turning to socialism, capitalists ceded to reformists who introduced changes to curb the market, control overproduction, and redistribute wealth.

The United States introduced progressive reforms with the New Deal, implementing parity prices, and land conservation, food, and work programs. (Germany and Italy turned to fascism.) After World War II, the widespread economic prosperity under strictly regulated capitalism had no historical precedent.[6] However, in the 1980s, under pressure from multinational corporations and the finance sectors, US President Ronald Reagan and UK Prime Minister Margaret Thatcher set about undoing New Deal reforms, ushering in the current phase of global neoliberalism.

When world financial markets crashed in 2008 and protests erupted around the world, many observers thought that reforms were imminent. Instead, with few exceptions, governments chose to bail out the banks rather than their citizens. Capitalism renewed its assault on the food system and the environment.

Why weren't social reforms instituted? All the

ingredients seemed to be present: a financial crash, widespread suffering, protests . . . What happened? In a nutshell: the counter-movements were too weak to threaten the existence of capitalism.

Ten years after the financial crisis, capitalism shows no indication of slowing down. On the contrary, extractive industries have redoubled their efforts to draw every last mineral, liter of gas, and drop of oil from the ground; industrial agriculture is expanding to new, more fragile land; and the retail industry is retooling and automating itself to function without workers, and inventing new products to address the dietary and environmental destruction in its wake.

But counter-movements have been growing too. Food, climate, and the rights of women, people of color, and indigenous peoples are in the forefront of a far-flung, diverse food movement. This "movement of movements" seeks transformational change. The movements for agroecology and food sovereignty are central to this effort.

Agroecology: resisting the corporate food regime

Agroecology arose as the science of sustainable agriculture in the 1980s to counter the socially and environmentally destructive trends of the Green Revolution. Notably, it emerged through the co-production of knowledge between farmers and scientists. At its core, it applied ecological concepts and principles to the design and management of sustainable agroecosystems.[7] This approach – grounded in the ecology of peasant food systems – came into conflict with the wider impacts of industrial agriculture. Agroecology's scope widened from farm to watershed scales, and then to the whole food system. It incorporated political economy into its focus in order to confront the social and political power of the corporate food regime. As one of its academic founders, Steve Gliessman, asserts:

> [Agroecology is] transdisciplinary in that it values all forms of knowledge and experience in food system change. It's participatory in that it requires the involvement of all stakeholders from the farm to the table and everyone in between. And it is action-oriented because it confronts the economic and political power structures of the current industrial food system with alternative social structures and policy action.[8]

In agroecology, farmers use primarily animal manures, legumes, and cover crops to provide nutrients. Weeds are controlled by cultivating, cover-cropping, inter-cropping, and mulching. Pests are managed by attracting predators with companion planting, interrupting pest cycles and vectors with rotations, alley-cropping, and the use of trap crops and repellant crops. Agroecology does not preclude small-scale mechanization to eliminate drudgery, but it requires the constant attention, skill, and inventiveness from the farmer. While some agroecological practices require more labor (especially in the beginning transition period before they are well established), many also reduce labor, or spread labor out more evenly over the agricultural year.

Though these represent just a sample of different agroecological management practices, they give an indication of why agroecology is anathema to capitalist agriculture: agroecology is knowledge-intensive (rather than capital-intensive) and doesn't provide opportunities for agribusiness to sell seeds, fertilizers, or pesticides.

Today, agroecology is taught in many universities and is the subject of a number of scientific journals. It is the preferred agricultural method for many non-governmental development projects and has been widely adopted by smallholders around the world. Agroecology has been endorsed by the IAASTD, and by the former United Nations Rapporteur on the Right to Food as the best agricultural method to end hunger, eliminate poverty, and address climate change. Agroecology is largely credited for helping Cuba rebuild its farming systems following the fall of the Soviet Union and the end of petroleum and fertilizer subsidies.

But agroecology is not a significant part of the agricultural development programs of the United States Agency for International Development (USAID), the Consultative Group on International Agricultural Research (CGIAR), the Alliance for a Green Revolution in Africa, the United Kingdom's Department for International Development (DFID), the World Bank, the Inter-American Development Bank, or African or Asian Development banks' plans for agricultural development. Funding for agroecological-oriented research in the National Science Foundation (NSF) in the United States represents less than 1 percent of the funding dedicated to industrial agriculture.

If agroecology is so great, why don't agricultural development institutions support it? The simple answer is because the objective of these institutions is the development, refinement, and spread of industrial agriculture and the expansion of opportunities for capitalist investment. Since agroecology reduces the ways that capital can appropriate the upstream activities of the food value chain, it works at cross purposes to capitalist agriculture.

Agroecology today is not only a science and a practice; it is also a social movement. In a report from the International Forum for Agroecology in 2015, the international peasant movement La Vía Campesina stated:

> Agroecology practiced by small scale producers generates local knowledge, promotes social justice, nurtures identity and culture and strengthens the economic viability of rural areas... [It] is political; it requires us to challenge and transform structures of power in society. We need to put the control of seeds, biodiversity, land and territories, waters, knowledge, culture and the commons in the hands of the peoples who feed the world.[9]

Since the early 1980s, hundreds of nongovernmental organizations (NGOs) in Africa, Latin America, and Asia have promoted thousands of agroecology projects that incorporate elements of traditional knowledge and modern agroecological science.[10] With the growing number of crises related to food, livelihoods, and climate, the importance of the social and environmental services provided by agroecological agriculture are becoming widely recognized.

While agroecology has spread widely through the efforts of NGOs, farmers' movements, and university projects, it remains marginal to government and multilateral efforts to end hunger or reverse climate change. In contrast, the remarkable spread of agroecology in countries like Cuba stems, in large part, from the government's strong structural support.[11] Asking "Why don't all farmers practice agroecology?" raises the question, "What is holding agroecology back?" The simple answer is capitalist agriculture.

Food security or food sovereignty?

People, communities, and households that experience hunger and malnutrition are typically described as being "food insecure." Food security is defined as: "[The] availability at all times of adequate world food supplies of basic foodstuffs to sustain a steady expansion of food consumption and to offset fluctuations in production and prices."[12] Food security exists when all people, at all times, have physical and economic access to sufficient, safe, and nutritious food to meet their dietary needs and food preferences for an active and healthy life. The "four pillars of food security are availability, access, utilization, and stability."[13]

The definition of food security does not address how food is grown, its nutritional value, who supplies this food, or how it is accessed. By this definition one can be food secure in jail. This is not an accident. Food from nowhere fits the global food system perfectly. This understanding of food security allows the Global North to dump its excess grain in the Global South, destroying local food systems but ostensibly making populations more food secure. When global food prices spike, as they did in 2008 and 2011, poor countries and poor households go hungry because they don't have a local food system to fall back on. Food security avoids addressing food dependency.

This is why the concept of food sovereignty was developed by La Vía Campesina, an international peasant, pastoralist, and fishers' organization with around 200 million members. Food sovereignty has been adopted as a guiding concept by thousands of organizations and social movements around the globe, notably by the World March of Women. Since its inception, food sovereignty has challenged neoliberal capitalism and the corporate food regime, and proposed structural policies such as land reform, the removal of food and agriculture from the World Trade Organization (WTO), the dismantling of agrifood monopolies, and an end to patriarchy and all violence against the majority of the world's farmers – women. As La Vía Campesina declared in 2007:

> Food sovereignty is the right of peoples to healthy and culturally appropriate food produced through ecologically sound and sustainable methods, and their right to define their own food and agriculture systems. It puts those who produce, distribute and consume food at the heart of food systems and policies rather than the demands of markets and corporations. It defends the interests and inclusion of the next generation. It offers a strategy to resist and dismantle the current corporate trade and food regime, and directions for food, farming, pastoral and fisheries systems determined by local producers. Food sovereignty prioritises local and national economies and markets and empowers peasant and family farmer-driven agriculture, artisanal fishing, pastoralist-led grazing, and food production, distribution and consumption based on environmental, social and economic sustainability.[14]

Can food sovereignty end hunger and environmental destruction?

Unlike food security, which is a technical term, food sovereignty is a political vision and a social movement, as well as a practice of resistance. Social movements and communities in the food sovereignty movement come in many forms. Some, like the food justice movement in the United States, may share principles but not the term itself. With the notable exception of the Zapatista indigenous communities in Chiapas, Mexico, there are very few autonomous islands of food sovereignty that control their own food systems.

There are many examples, however, of food sovereignty principles that, when put into practice, contribute to the construction of food sovereignty. In the Basque Country of the Iberian Peninsula, the Basque Farmer's Union (EHNE-Bizkaia) developed a network of community-supported agriculture (CSA). Each farmer supplied a basket of vegetables to thirty urban families. When strong north winds blew down one farmer's greenhouse, ruining his crops, he received a weekly basket of vegetables donated by thirty other farmers in EHNE. His CSA members received their food and the farmer received his weekly income. On the weekends, CSA members and EHNE members helped the farmer reconstruct his greenhouse. The Basque Farmer's Union built solidarity and equity into its CSA network, foundational to food sovereignty. Farmer Esti Redondo affirmed:

> Food Sovereignty is a right and a utopia that helps us change society. It is the right of all peoples to decide on their means of production and what they eat. In order for this right to exist, we must change all the social and political structures we have today. It is a struggle against the system and a struggle for good livelihoods.[15]

Frances Moore Lappé and Joseph Collins describe similar experiences from around the world of communities pushing back against the corporate food regime, advancing alternatives, taking control over their food and their lives, bit by bit.[16]

- The village of Punukula in the Indian state of Anwar Pradesh went from being the "pesticide capital" of India with dozens of farmer pesticide poisoning every year, to becoming completely pesticide-free. Farmers weaned themselves off pesticide with natural, local products (like neem), then taught others through a far-flung network of farmer field schools that reaches 12,000 villages and 2 million small farms on their way to becoming pesticide-free.
- Navdanya, a women's seed-saving collective in the state of Uttarakhand, India launched the Bida Satyagraha (Seed Freedom) movement that blocked patents on the ubiquitous neem tree.

They have conserved over 3,000 rice varieties from across India, as well as lentils, wheat, and other cultivars. More than half a million farmers are in the movement, leading Uttarakhand to declare itself "an organic state."

- The Brazilian Landless Workers Movement (MST) has mobilized hundreds of thousands of landless farmworkers to take the Brazilian constitution at its word: they invade idle lands that were not "performing a social function," effectively implementing their own land reform. The MST has carried out over 2,500 occupations and settled over a million families on the land. Over 2,000 schools serving 150,000 children and 3,000 adults have been started on the new MST farms. Special agroecology schools are providing training for farm families. The MST's impact has gone far beyond its farms. As one of the main organizations of the Brazilian food sovereignty movement, it was instrumental in putting the Brazilian Workers Party into power, and pushed for state-sponsored reforms that included the highly successful Fome Zero (Zero Hunger) program.

Lappé and Collins document many other experiences on the road to food sovereignty, most of which also include agroecology as a component of struggle, including the Campesino a Campesino Movement of Latin America; the agroforesty successes of Tigray, Ethiopia, Burkina Faso, and Malawi; the amazing effectiveness of sustainable rice intensification across Africa; and the citizens' juries made up of farmers that are holding agribusiness accountable in West Africa, Asia, and Brazil. La Vía Campesina has adopted agroecology as its agricultural approach for the implementation of food sovereignty.

Groundswell International, a grassroots agricultural development agency, has documented farmer-managed natural regeneration (FMNR) across Western Africa, as well as farmer-led agroecology movements in Honduras, Brazil, Haiti, and Ecuador.[17] The United States and Europe and Australia are hosts to a growing permaculture movement that is spreading throughout Latin America and other parts of the world.

These diverse experiences are just a few examples of the articulation between agroecology and food sovereignty. What is striking about this convergence is not only that people insist on controlling their food and protecting their environments around the world, but that, despite their lack of resources, they are gaining ground from within a food regime that is antithetical to their struggle.[18] But will they be able to build a global counter-movement strong enough (and quickly enough) to transform the food system before it is too late? Perhaps – but there are some formidable challenges.

Changing everything: food, capitalism, and the challenges of our time

To feed the world without destroying it, we need to build an alternative to the capitalist food system, which means building an alternative to capitalism itself. This is a big political project that has been attempted in the past with only partial success (and some disastrous results). Capitalism does not take kindly to systemic challenges. Nonetheless, it is fruitless to keep insisting on minor adjustments to a system that has become toxic to life on earth. Luckily, the food system is well positioned in this regard. How we produce and consume determines how our society is organized. But how we organize socially and politically can also determine how we produce and consume. The question is not whether we can end hunger without replacing capitalism, but how a powerful food movement might catalyze society to demand the deep systemic reforms upon which our collective future depends.

Who *Can* Feed the World Without Destroying It?

When we assess the potential for different approaches to end poverty, hunger, and malnutrition, or to reverse global warming and environmental destruction, we must also ask how these strategies will affect the relations of power in our food system. Do they challenge the status quo or accommodate it? Are they regressive or redistributive? Will they concentrate power within the halls of unaccountable corporate control, or work to decentralize and democratize our food system in favor of the poor? Will they strengthen or weaken social movements? Do these approaches simply mitigate the externalities of the corporate food regime, or actually help us transcend the regime itself?

By themselves, it is unlikely that the food sovereignty and agroecology movements can build enough power to transform the food regime. They will need to unite with other groups seeking progressive social and economic change, like the indigenous movement, the climate justice movement, and the women's movement. These broad alliances are crucial to building movement power, as are alliances with movements for radical democracy, de-growth, and trade reform. This convergence is well under way, but it faces serious challenges.

To begin with, the nature of counter-movements and the threats to capitalism are very different today than they were in the 1930s. Rather than being defined and led by labor and progressive political parties, today's embryonic counter-movement is made up of a diverse range of interests representing indigenous communities, environmentalists, feminists, peasants and family farmers, food workers, farmworkers, people of color, immigrants, and young people. The biggest threat to capitalism today is not communism, but the possibility of ungovernability resulting from a deadly combination of poverty, hunger, climate disasters, and mass migrations. In addition, as the rise of neo fascist movements around the world illustrates, we cannot rule out the threat of a reactionary, totalitarian response to the grinding crises of capitalism. Building a powerful, progressive food movement is part of a much larger political struggle for democracy, equity, and systems transformation.

The historical divisions of racism, classism, and sexism have been exacerbated by the neoliberal shrinking of the state and the erosion of the public sphere. Not only have the social functions of government been gutted; also, social networks within communities have been weakened, increasing levels of violence, intensifying racial tensions, and deepening cultural divides. People are challenged to confront the problems of hunger, violence, poverty, and climate change in an environment in which society has been restructured to serve global markets rather than local communities.[19] To engage effectively under these circumstances, economist Samir Amin proposes a strategy of "convergence in diversity," combined with a critical "repoliticization" of social movements. This means not only building alternative practices and markets to the capitalist food system, but politically replacing the regressive structures of capitalism with economically democratic, progressive, and redistributive forms of governance.[20]

Work in the public sphere is essential to this task. Global elites are well aware of this. They meet yearly in Davos, Switzerland at the World Economic Forum, the world's most exclusive "public sphere." Here, the likes of Monsanto, Syngenta, Exxon, Walmart, and other monopolies come together with billionaire philanthro-capitalists and multilateral institutions like the International Monetary Fund and the World Bank to discuss the future of capitalism.

What is needed is a critical public sphere so that the majorities – rather than the elites – can formulate strategies and take the actions urgently needed to end hunger, reverse climate change, and transform our political-economic systems.

112

Who *Can* Feed the World Without Destroying It?

These critical public spheres are already in construction, and are increasingly crossing borders, languages, cultures, and classes. They are growing. The World Social Forum (WSF) was started in 2001 in opposition to the World Economic Forum. The WSF has met fifteen times, preceded by dozens of national social forums each year. Hundreds of thousands of people attend from around the world. La Vía Campesina and its 200 million members hold national, regional, and global gatherings to advance the cause of food sovereignty. In the United States, Canada, and Australia, hundreds of food policy councils have been working to democratically change the rules and the institutions of local food systems. Civil society has built a strong public presence in consultative spaces of the FAO. Community-supported agriculture, local food policy councils, and thousands of farm to school programs are bypassing the industrial agrifoods system, building democratic spaces of decision making within the food system.

Consciously or not, in many ways the hands-on, participatory projects for a fair, sustainable, healthy food are also rebuilding our public sphere from the ground up. But do they go far enough? Do the projects for community gardens also result in politically organized community groups that pressure city councils for redistributive forms of property?

Do farmer field schools train and link community leaders to demand rights to agricultural research services, water, and land? Do food policy councils also provide social platforms to address labor rights, racism, and sexism in the food system? Does the revival of the Grange (an historical US agrarian society) and of land trusts and land banks also address the need for agrarian reform? Are fair food and workers' rights groups linking their work with immigrant rights? The challenge is to articulate and politicize these efforts.

For much of the food movement, this means assuming the politics of the community work they are already doing. Progressive agroecological, good food, and food justice activists need to keep working to change the practices of our food system. The radical food sovereignty organizations calling for an end to seed, chemical, and food monopolies, taking food out of the WTO, and the implementation of agrarian reform need to continue their political work to change the structures of our food system. When the work of progressives and radicals of the food movement come together, and when the food movement builds alliances with the climate justice movement, the women's movement, the immigrant rights movement, and other movements for liberation, the anticapitalist counter-movement will be strong enough to force deep, transformative reforms upon the food regime.

What specific policies should these movements come together to change? The long, context-specific list can be loosely grouped in areas of regulation, public support, and grassroots movement building. As the International Panel of Experts on Sustainable Food Systems proposes, this includes (but is by no means limited to): shifting resources in agricultural development, education, and research institutions to support diversified agroecological production systems and bring agroecology into the mainstream; supporting short (local) supply chains and alternative retail infrastructures; and supporting local food planning processes and restorative, equitable, and sustainable food projects and policies at multiple levels.[21] This is not a call for autarchy, nor an end to international trade, but a shift toward building subsidiarity – that is, producing and controlling as much as is socially and environmentally possible at local scales.

A few fundamental, structural guidelines seem evident.

First, the environmental and social costs of producing food need to be internalized into the price of food, including all forms of soil, water, and atmospheric pollution on a "polluter pays" principle. If food and farm workers were paid living wages and ensured decent working conditions free of exploitation and chemical poisoning, this would not only be a disincentive to most of the destructive practices of industrial agriculture, it would help level the economic playing field between large, industrial operations (that tend to externalize these costs) and smaller, labor and knowledge-intensive operations. It would create more jobs and help keep wealth in the countryside. Further, if farmers were given economic support based on sustainable production quotas (and limits), and paid a parity price for their product, this would end overproduction and provide an incentive for them to use the least amount of chemical inputs on their farms. That parity price needn't be excessive if farm communities were guaranteed a decent social wage through targeted public investment in health, education, and welfare in the countryside. Incentives and public projects for a massive environmental restoration effort will reverse greenhouse gas (GHG) emissions in agriculture, provide jobs, and restore fertility to degraded soils and agroecosystems. The technological paradigm needs to shift from "high-tech" to a "wide-tech" focus on diversified, decentralized knowledge and innovation, and open access technologies.[22] All this would turn the countryside from a toxic wasteland and a backwater of poverty into a healthy, desirable place for sustainable livelihoods.

Second, the power of food, agriculture, and chemical monopolies must be dismantled, with a focus on protecting family farmers as well as consumers. While this can start with the actual enforcement of existing antitrust laws, it needs to be accompanied by incentives for decentralized operations throughout the food system, including the redistribution of concentrated land and resources not serving a social and environmental purpose. Unfair practices in supply chains and sector-wide consolidation in the food sector should be given special scrutiny in the food and agriculture sector, and food should be treated as a special commodity to which everyone has a right.

Incentives and protections for social ownership and democratic governance of food system resources such as land, water, and markets, should be implemented. New technologies (like nanotechnology and Big Data) need to be regulated on the basis of their impact on corporate consolidation as well as their environmental impact. Pesticide companies should not own seed companies; farm machinery companies should not control chemicals, seeds, or crop insurance. An international treaty on competition and consolidation should be negotiated. Laws against financial speculation in food, land, water, and natural resources and the justiciable right to food should be adopted and enforced internationally.

It is unclear just how long we have to make the profound changes we need for our food systems, but by all indications it is a matter of decades. While the desired characteristics are emerging, we don't know exactly what forms these transformations will ultimately take. We do know what will happen if we continue with the corporate food regime: massive hunger and socio-environmental collapse. It will take the local and global strength of allied social movements to put our political and economic institutions on the path to healing the planet and ending hunger.

Successful social movements are formed by integrating activism with livelihoods. These integrated movements create the sustained social pressure that produces political will – the key to changing the political-economic structures that presently work against sustainability and equity.

Who can feed the world without destroying it? We can – by changing everything.

Further Reading

The literature on food, hunger, and the environment is vast and growing daily. Most of this work follows Amartya Sen's foundational *Poverty and Famines: An Essay on Entitlement and Deprivation* (Clarendon Press, 1982), which demonstrates that modern famines are not the result of scarcity and do not occur under democratic governments. Frances Moore Lappé's evergreen book *Diet for a Small Planet* (Ballantine Books, 1971) applied a non-scarcity framework to both food and the environment and called out developed countries for eating too high on the food chain. This was followed by *World Hunger: Twelve Myths* (Grove Press, 1986), written with Joseph Collins; Peter Rosset (with Luis Esparza) joined Lappé and Collins in 1998 with a second revised edition, in which the authors deepened and extended the framework, asserting that people can feed themselves if given the chance. Lappé and Collins later wrote *World Hunger: Ten Myths* (Grove Press/Food First Books, 2015), which provides many examples of how communities end hunger by taking back control over the food systems in a process the authors call "food democracy."

Raj Patel's *Stuffed and Starved* (Melville House, 2008) brings the issues of health and overconsumption to bear on hunger and environmental destruction. Patel is also coauthor, with this author and Annie Shattuck, of *Food Rebellions: Crisis and the Hunger for Justice* (Pambazooka Press/Food First Books, 2009), which analyzes the structural causes of the 2008 food crisis, reviews the false solutions being advanced by governments, big philanthropy, multilateral agencies, and the food industry, and introduces the alternative approaches challenging the corporate food regime. More targeted works in this critical vein include: David Rieff's *The Reproach of Hunger: Food, Justice, and Money in the Twenty-first Century* (Simon & Schuster, 2015), which calls out the false optimism of big philanthropy and celebrity activism; *The Conquest of Bread: 150 Years of Agribusiness in California* (The New Press, 2004) by Richard Walker, which documents the emblematic rise of agribusiness and the supermarket model in California; *Foodopoly: The Battle Over the Future of Food and Farming in America* (The New Press, 2014) by Wenona Hauter, which analyzes the growing – and unaccountable – monopoly power of agrifoods corporations; Andy Fisher's *Big Hunger: The Unholy Alliance Between Corporate America and Anti-Hunger Groups* (MIT Press, 2017), which exposes how the ostensible largesse of food monopolies actually perpetuates hunger; and *The Ecological Hoofprint: The Global Burden of Industrial Livestock* (Zed Books, 2013) by Tony Weis, and *Big Farms Make Big Flu: Dispatches on Infectious Disease, Agribusiness, and the Nature of Science* (Monthly Review, 2016) by Rob Wallace, both of which show how the rise of industrial meat is at the heart of environmental destruction and the food-based pandemics sweeping the globe.

The areas of agroecology and agricultural development are also extensive. Foundational works include: *Good Farmers: Traditional Agricultural Resource Management in Mexico and Central America* (University of California Press, 1988) by Gene Wilken; *Agroecology: The Scientific Basis of Sustainable Agriculture* (Westview Press, 1987) by Miguel Altieri; and *Two Ears of Corn: A Guide to People-Centered Agricultural Improvement* (World Neighbors, 1985) by Roland Bunch. Wilken's book is rich in case studies of traditional farmers;

Altieri defines the science of sustainable agriculture; while Bunch documents the effectiveness of peer-driven agricultural development. These books lay the groundwork for the farmers' movements documented by this author in *Campesino a Campesino: Voices from Latin America's Farmer to Farmer Movement for Sustainable Agriculture* (Food First Books, 2006). *Food Sovereignty: Reconnecting Food, Nature and Community* (Fernwood Press, 2010) by Annette Desmarais, Hannah Wittman, and Nettie Wiebe brings out the voices of this remarkable global peasant movement. For a completely different take on the political economy of food systems, *China's Peasant Agriculture and Rural Society: Changing Paradigms of Farming*, edited by Jan Douwe van der Ploeg and Jingzhong Ye (Routledge/Earthscan, 2017), stands out as an account from a country whose society and government are poorly understood in the West.

Readings that address the political ecology of food systems include Cary McWilliams's classic, *Factories in the Field: The Story of Migratory Farm Labor in California* (University of California, 1935); *Agriculture and Food in Crisis: Conflict, Resistance, and Renewal*, edited by Fred Magdoff and Brian Tokar (Monthly Review, 2010); *The Breakfast of Biodiversity: The Political Ecology of*

Further Reading

Rain Forest Destruction (Food First Books, 2005) by John Vandermeer and Ivette Perfecto; and *Nature's Matrix: Linking Agriculture, Conservation and Food Sovereignty* (Earthscan, 2009) by Ivette Perfecto, John Vandermeer, and Angus Wright. These works provide a trenchant, biologically grounded analysis to the political economy of food production and environmental destruction.

The toughest nut to crack are books with an accessible, working knowledge of capitalism. David Harvey provides the most accessible, comprehensive contemporary guide to the classic works of Karl Marx with his online course and *A Companion to Marx's Capital* (Verso, 2010). You will have to actually read Marx's *Capital*, though! Karl Polanyi's *The Great Transformation: The Political and Economic Origins of Our Time* (Beacon Press, 2001) is foundational reading for understanding today's neoliberalism and the historical tendency towards "counter-movements" to capitalism's excesses. *A Foodie's Guide to Capitalism: Understanding the Political Economy of What We Eat* by this author (Monthly Review Press/Food First Books, 2017) provides a more in-depth and historical assessment of many of the themes addressed in this book.

Notes

Chapter 1 *The Politics, Power, and Potential of Food*

1 A food regime is a rule-governed structure of production and consumption of food on a world scale. The first global food regime (1870–1930s) was rooted in British hegemony and a system of free trade imperialism. Cheap food and raw materials from the tropical and temperate settler colonies fueled industrialization in Europe. The second food regime (1950s–1970s) reversed the flow of food from South to North that had characterized the first regime as a transfer of US agricultural surpluses to the South began in the form of food aid. The Green Revolution, the Third World debt crisis and ensuing structural adjustment programs, and the dumping of Northern surplus in the Global South turned the South's $1 billion/year surplus of food to an $11 billion/year deficit, making it dependent on the North for much of its food. The current "corporate food regime" (1980s to the

present) emerged from the global economic shocks of the 1970s and 1980s, which ushered in the current "globalization" period of neoliberal capitalist expansion, the World Trade Organization (WTO) and regional free trade agreements (FTAs). The corporate food regime is also characterized by a "supermarket revolution" and the meteoric rise of food retail giants, the consolidation of the seed and grain markets under monopoly control, and the appearance of biofuels and the industrial grain–oilseed–livestock complex. See Eric Holt-Giménez and Annie Shattuck, "Food Crises, Food Regimes and Food Movements: Rumblings of Reform or Tides of Transformation?" *Journal of Peasant Studies* 38, no. 1 (January 2011): 109–44.

Chapter 2   Hunger in a World of Plenty

1 "Millennium Development Goals Report 2015" (New York: United Nations, 2015), http://www. un.org/millenniumgoals/2015_MDG_Report/pdf/ MDG%202015%20rev%20%28July%201%29. pdf.

2 FAO, IFAD, UNICEF, WFP, and WHO, "The State of Food Security and Nutrition in the World 2017: Building Resilience for Peace and Food Security" (Rome: FAO), http://www.fao.org/3/a-I7695e.pdf.

3 Eric Holt-Giménez, "The True Extent of Hunger: What the FAO Isn't Telling You," Backgrounder (Oakland, CA: Food First Books/Institute for Food and Development Policy, 2016), https://foodfirst.

org/wp-content/uploads/2016/06/Summer2016Back grounder.pdf.

4 Jason Hickel, "The True Extent of Global Poverty and Hunger: Questioning the Good News Narrative of the Millennium Development Goals," *Third World Quarterly* 37, no. 5 (May 3, 2016): 749–67, https://doi.org/10.1080/01436597.2015.1109 439.

5 "Rome Declaration on World Food Security" (Rome: FAO, 1996), http://www.fao.org/wfs/index_ en.htm.

6 Millennium Summit, "Millennium Declaration," September 2000, www.visitmorocco.com.

7 Philip McMichael and Mindi Schneider, "Food Security Politics and the Millennium Development Goals," *Third World Quarterly* 32, no. 1 (February 1, 2011): 119–39, https://doi.org/10.1080/01436597 .2011.543818.

8 Thomas Pogge, "The First United Nations Millennium Development Goal: A Cause for Celebration?," *Journal of Human Development* 5, no. 3 (2004): 377–97.

9 Hickel, "The True Extent of Global Poverty and Hunger."

10 Martin Caparros, "Counting the Hungry," *New York Times*, September 27, 2014, http://www. nytimes. com/2014/09/28/opinion/sunday/counting-the-hungry.html?_r=0.

11 Eric Holt-Giménez, Raj Patel, and Annie Shattuck, *Food Rebellions: Crisis and the Hunger for*

Justice (Oakland, CA/Oxford: Food First Books/ Pambazooka Press, 2009).

12 "Millennium Development Goals Report 2013" (New York: United Nations, 2013).

13 "State of Food Insecurity in the World 2012. Rome: FAO, 2012" (Rome: FAO, 2012).

14 Frances Moore Lappé et al., "Framing Hunger: A Response to the State of Food Insecurity in the World 2012," June 2013, http://www.ase. tufts.edu/gdae/ pubs/rp/framinghunger.pdf.

15 Moore Lappé et al.

16 UNDP, "Sustainable Development Goals" (United Nations Development Program, 2016), http://www. undp.org/content/undp/en/home/sustainable-devel opment-goals.html.

17 See Frances Moore Lappé, Joseph Collins, and Peter Rosset, *World Hunger: Twelve Myths*, 2nd ed (New York: Grove Press, Food First Books, 1998), 12 (1st ed. 1986).

18 Frances Moore Lappé and Joseph Collins, *World Hunger: Ten Myths* (New York/Oakland: Grove Press Food First Books, 2015).

19 Isobel Tomlinson, "Doubling Food Production to Feed the 9 Billion: A Critical Perspective on a Key Discourse of Food Security in the UK," *Journal of Rural Studies* 29 (2013): 81–90.

20 Douglas Boucher, "Humanity's 'Need' for 'Food' in 2050," *Blog of Union of Concerned Scientists*, August 18, 2015, https://blog.ucsusa.org/doug-bou cher/humanitys-need-for-food-in-2050-848.

21 Eric Holt-Giménez et al., "We Already Grow Enough

Food for 10 Billion People . . . and Still Can't End Hunger," *Journal of Sustainable Agriculture* 36, no. 6 (2012): 595–98.

22 GRAIN, "Hungry for Land: Small Farmers Feed the World with Less than a Quarter of All Farmland" (Barcelona: GRAIN, May 2014), http://www.grain. org/article/entries/4929-hungry-for-land-small-farm ers-feed-the-world-with-less-than-a-quarter-of-all- farmland.

23 Eric Holt-Giménez, *A Foodie's Guide to Capitalism: Understanding the Political Economy of What We Eat* (New York: Monthly Review Press/Food First Books, 2017).

24 In the United States and Europe direct farm pay- ments, environmental subsidies, price supports, pro- tective tariffs, and export assistance total more than $300 billion a year – almost the GDP of the entire African continent and *six times* the amount of OECD development assistance to the Global South (FAO 2002).

25 Eric Holt-Giménez, Justine Williams, and Caitlyn Hachmyer, "The World Bank Group's 2013–15 Agriculture for Action Plan: A Lesson in Privatization, Lack of Oversight and Tired Development Paradigms," Development Report (Oakland, CA: Food First Books/Institute for Food and Development Policy, October 2015), https://foodfirst.org/publication/ the-world-bank-groups-2013-15-agriculture-for- action-plan-a-lesson-in-privatization-lack-of-over sight-and-tired-development-paradigms/.

26 This section is based on: Holt-Giménez, Patel, and

Shattuck, *Food Rebellions: Crisis and the Hunger for Justice.*

27 Lappé, Collins, and Rosset, *World Hunger: Twelve Myths.*

28 World Bank, "The CGIAR at 31: An Independent Meta-Evaluation of the Consultative Group on International Agricultural Research" (World Bank Group, 2003), 31.

29 C. Hewitt de Alcántara, *Modernizing Mexican Agriculture* (Geneva: United Nations Research Institute for Social Development, 1976). S. R. Gliessman, *Agroecology: Ecological Processes in Sustainable Agriculture* (Chelsea: Ann Arbor Press, 1998). V. Shiva, *The Violence of the Green Revolution*, ed. T.W. network (London: Zed Books, 1991). *The Ecologist*, "CGIAR Agricultural Research for Whom?" December 1996

30 B. Jennings, *Foundations of International Agricultural Research: Science and Politics in Mexican Agriculture* (Boulder, CO: Westview Press, 1988). Donald K. Freebairn, "Did the Green Revolution Concentrate Incomes? A Quantitative Study of Research Report," *World Development* 23, no. 2 (1973): 265–79.

31 Raj Patel, "The Long Green Revolution," *Journal of Peasant Studies* 40, no. 1 (January 1, 2013): 1–63, https://doi.org/10.1080/03066150.2012.719224.

32 Boston Consulting Group, *The Next Billions: Business Strategies to Enhance Food Value Chains and Empower the Poor* (Geneva: World Economic Forum, 2009).

33 Sally Brooks, *Rice Biofortification: Lessons for*

Global Science and Development (London: Earthscan Publications, 2010).

34 Klaus von Grebmer et al., "The Challenge of Hidden Hunger," Global Hunger Index (Bonn/Washington DC/Dublin: International Food Policy Research Institute, October 2014), 3.

35 Brooks, *Rice Biofortification*.

36 Elanita C. Daño, "Biofortification: Trojan horse of Corporate Food Control?" *Development* 57, No. 2 (December 2014): 201–9.

37 Daño, "Biofortification."

38 GAIN, "Public–Private Partnership Launched to Improve Nutrition in Developing Countries," Global Alliance for Improved Nutrition, *First Annual Forum of the Business Alliance for Food Fortification* (blog), 2005, http://www.gainhealth.org/knowledge-centre/ first-annual-forum-business-alliance-food-fortifica tion/.

39 George Scrinis, *Nutritionism: The Science and Politics of Dietary Advice* (New York: Columbia University Press, 2013).

40 Tristam Stewart, *Waste: Uncovering the Global Food Scandal* (New York: Norton, 2009).

41 Dana Gunders, "Wasted: How America Is Losing Up to 40 Percent of Its Food From Farm to Fork to Landfill" (National Resources Defense Council, August 2012), https://www.nrdc.org/sites/default/ files/wasted-food-IP.pdf.

42 Brian Lipinski et al., "Reducing Food Loss and Waste," Working Paper (Washington, DC: World Resources Institute, May 2013), http://www.wri.org/

sites/default/files/reducing_food_loss_and_waste.
pdf.
43 Gunders, "Wasted."
44 "USDA and EPA Join with Private Sector, Charitable
Organizations to Set Nation's First Food Waste
Reduction Goals," https://www.usda.gov/oce/food-
waste/.

Chapter 3 Food, Environment, and Systems Change

1 Donella H. Meadows, Dennis L. Meadows, Jorgen
Randers, and William W. Behrens III. *The Limits to
Growth: Report from the Club of Rome's Project on
the Predicament of Mankind* (New York: Universe
Books, 1972).
2 Parenti Christian, "'The Limits to Growth': A
Book That Launched a Movement," *The Nation*,
December 2012, https://www.thenation.com/article/
limits-growth-book-launched-movement/.
3 Johan Rockstrom et al., "Planetary Boundaries:
Exploring the Safe Operating Space for Humanity,"
Ecology and Society 14, no. 2 (2009), http://www.
ecologyandsociety.org/vol14/iss2/art32/.
4 Murray Bookchin, *Remaking Society* (Portland, OR:
Black Rose Books, 1989).
5 "[The] soil washed away from the high land in these
periodical catastrophes forms no alluvial deposit of
consequence as in other places but is carried out and
lost in the deeps. You are left ... with something
rather like the skeleton of a body wasted by disease; the rich, soft soil has all run away leaving the

land nothing but skin and bone." Plato, *Timaeus and Critias*, trans. Desmond Lee (New York: Penguin, 1977).

6 Dale T. Carter, *Topsoil and Civilization* (Norman, OK: University of Oklahoma Press, 1955).

7 Fred Magdoff and John Bellamy Foster, "Liebig, Marx and the Depletion of Soil Fertility: Relevance for Today's Agriculture," in *Hungry for Profit: The Agribusiness Threat to Farmers, Food and the Environment* (New York: Monthly Review Press, 2000).

8 Karl Marx, *Capital: A Critique of Political Economy*, vol. 1 (New York: International Publishers, 1967), 637–38.

9 Fred Magdoff and Chris Williams, *Creating an Ecological Society: Toward a Revolutionary Transformation* (New York: Monthly Review Press, 2017).

10 Magdoff and Foster, "Liebig, Marx and the Depletion of Soil Fertility."

11 Fred Magdoff, "A Rational Agriculture Is Incompatible with Capitalism," *Monthly Review* 66, no. 10 (March 2015): 1–18.

12 John Ikerd, "The New Farm Crisis Calls for New Farm Policy" (Missouri Farmers' Union Annual Conference, Jefferson City, MO, 2002), http://web.missouri.edu/ikerdj/papers/FarmUnion.pdf.

13 Stacy Noel, "Economics of Land Degradation Initiative: Report for Policy and Decision Makers" (Bonn, Germany: ELD Initiative, September 2015), http://www.eld-initiative.org/fileadmin/pdf/ELD-pm-report_05_web_300dpi.pdf.

14 Naomi Stewart, "The Value of Land: Prosperous Lands and Positive Rewards through Sustainable Land Management," ELD Initiative (Bonn, Germany: ELD Initiative, 2015), http://eld-initiative. org/fileadmin/pdf/ELD-main-report_05_web_72dpi. pdf.

15 Magdoff and Williams, *Creating an Ecological Society*.

16 Denise Breitburg et al., "Declining Oxygen in the Global Ocean and Coastal Waters," *Science* 359, no. 6371 (January 5, 2018), https://doi.org/10.1126/science.aam7240.

17 Dennis Dimick, "If You Think the Water Crisis Can't Get Worse, Wait Until the Aquifers Are Drained," *National Geographic*, August 21, 2014.

18 David Biello, "Is Northwestern India's Breadbasket Running Out of Water?," *Scientific American*, August 12, 2009, https://www.scientificamerican. com/article/is-india-running-out-of-water/.

19 Eric Holt-Giménez, "Measuring Farmers' Agroecological Resistance to Hurricane Mitch in Central America" (International Institute for Environment and Development, 2001).

20 Stacy Philpott et al., "A Multi-Scale Assessment of Hurricane Impacts on Agricultural Landscapes Based on Land Use and Topographic Features," *Agriculture, Ecosystems & Environment* 123, no. 1–2 (2008): 12–20, http://www.sciencedirect.com/science/article/pii/s0167880908001382.

21 Hallman Caspar, "More than 75 Percent Decline over 27 Years in Total Flying Insect Biomass in Protected

Areas," *PLOS ONE*, 2017, https://doi.org/10.1371/journal.pone.0185809.

22 IPCC, "IPCC Fourth Assessment Report: Climate Change. 4: Adaptation and Mitigation Options" (Intergovernmental Panel on Climate Change, 2007), https://www.ipcc.ch/publications_and_data/ar4/syr/en/spms4.html.

23 Henning Steinfeld et al., *Livestock's Long Shadow: Environmental Issues and Options* (Food and Agriculture Organization of the United Nations, 2006).

24 Nicolas Stern, "The Stern Review on the Economics of Climate Change" (London: UK Office of the Exchequer, 2006).

25 Annie Shattuck, "Food, Climate and the Myths That Keep Our Planet Hot," Backgrounder, Climate Justice (Oakland, CA: Food First Books/Institute for Food and Development Policy, 2017), https://foodfirst.org/publication/food-climate-and-the-myths-that-keep-our-planet-hot/.

26 FUNDESCA, *El Último Despale... La Frontera Agrícola Centroamericana* (San José, Costa Rica: Fundación para el Desarrollo Económico y Social de Centro América, 1994).

27 Sam Lawson, "Consumer Goods and Deforestation: An Analysis of the Extent and Nature of Illegality in Forest Conversion for Agriculture and Timber Plantations," *Forest Trends* (2014), http://www.forest-trends.org/illegal-deforestation.php.

28 Tony Weis, *The Ecological Hoofprint: The Global*

Burden of Industrial Livestock (London: Zed Books, 2013).

29 Tony Weis, "Towards 120 Billion: Dietary Change and Animal Lives," *Radical Philosophy*, October 2016, https://www.radicalphilosophy.com/commentary/towards-120-billion.

30 Biological speed-up in salmon production has moved from intensified sea harvest to intensive caged farming of genetically modified, inland farmed fish. The patented *AquAdvantage* salmon combines genes from the Chinook and Atlantic salmon with the ocean pout, a fast-growing eel-like fish, reducing production time "from egg to plate" from three years to eighteen months. Genetically engineered "salmon" grown largely on fish meal in Panamanian grown ponds will soon be being shipped around the world.

31 Weis, "Towards 120 Billion."

32 Gordon Conway, *The Doubly Green Revolution* (London: Penguin Books, 1997).

33 Ismail Serageldin, "The CGIAR at Twenty-Five: Into the Future," in *International Centers Week, October 28–November* (Washington, DC: CGIAR, 1997).

34 Gordon Conway, *One Billion Hungry : Can We Feed the World?* (Ithaca, NY: Cornell University Press, 2012).

35 Eric Holt-Giménez, "*One Billion Hungry: Can We Feed the World?* by Gordon Conway. (Book Review)," *Agroecology and Sustainable Food Systems* 37, no. 8 (2013): 968–71.

36 Peter Rosset, "The Multiple Functions and Benefits of Small Farm Agriculture in the Context of Global

Trade Negotiations," Food First Policy Brief (Oakland, CA: Food First Books/Institute for Food and Development Policy, 1999).

37 Sylvia Kantor, "Comparing Yields with Land Equivalent Ratio (LER)," Agriculture and Natural Resources Fact Sheet (Renton, Washington: Washington State University, King County, 2017), https://ay14-15.moodle.wisc.edu/prod/pluginfile. php/59463/mod_resource/content/0/LERfactsheet. pdf.

38 C. Badgley et al., "Organic Agriculture and the Global Food Supply," *Renewable Agriculture and Food Systems* 22, no. 2 (2007): 86–108. Jules Pretty and Rachel Hine, "Feeding the World with Sustainable Agriculture: A Summary of New Evidence," Final Report from SAFE-World Research Project (Colchester: University of Essex, 2000). E. Holt-Giménez, "Measuring Farmers' Agroecological Resistance after Hurricane Mitch in Nicaragua: A Case Study in Participatory, Sustainable Land Management Impact Monitoring," *Agriculture, Ecosystems & Environment* 93 (2002): 87–105.

39 E.O. Wilson and Robert MacArthur, *The Theory of Island Biogeography* (Princeton, NJ: Princeton University Press, 1967).

40 John Vandermeer, Ivette Perfecto, and Angus Wright, *Nature's Matrix: Linking Agriculture, Conservation and Food Sovereignty* (London: Earthscan, 2009).

41 Claire Kremen, "Reframing the Land-Sparing/Land-Sharing Debate for Biodiversity Conservation," *Annals of the New York Academy of Sciences*

1355, no. 1 (October 1, 2015): 52–76, https://doi. org/10.1111/nyas.12845.

42 Claire Kremen, "How to Feed the World Without Killing the Planet," University of California, Berkeley, *Cool Green Science* (blog), July 14, 2017, https:// blog.nature.org/science/2017/07/07/feed-world-with out-killing-planet-agriculture-food-security/.

43 George Naylor, "Agricultural Parity for Land De-Commodification," in Justine M. Williams and Eric Holt-Giménez, eds., *Land Justice: Re-Imagining Land, Food and the Commons in the United States* (Oakland, CA: Food First Books, 2017).

44 Marcus Taylor, "Climate-Smart Agriculture: What Is It Good For?," *Journal of Peasant Studies* 45, no. 1 (January 2, 2018): 89–107, https://doi.org/10.1080/ 03066150.2017.1312355.

45 Madeleine Fairbairn, "'Like Gold with Yield'. Evolving Intersections between Farmland and Finance," *The Journal of Peasant Studies* 41, no. 5 (September 3, 2014): 777–95, https://doi.org/10.108 0/03066150.2013.873977.

46 Lorenz Cotula and Thierry Berger, "Trends in Global Land Use Investment: Implications for Legal Empowerment" (London, 2017), http://pubs.iied. org/pdfs/12606IIED.pdf.

47 OXFAM, "The Truth about Land Grabs," ND, https://www.oxfamamerica.org/take-action/cam paign/food-farming-and-hunger/land-grabs/.

48 William Ripple and et al., "World Scientists' Warning to Humanity: A Second Notice," *BioScience* 67, no. 12 (2017): 1026–28.

Chapter 4   Who Can Feed the World Without Destroying It?

1 Joseph A. Schumpeter, *Capitalism, Socialism and Democracy* (London and New York: Routledge, 1976).

2 Beverly McIntire et al., "Agriculture at a Crossroads: International Assessment of Agricultural Knowledge, Science and Technology for Development," Synthesis (Washington, DC: Island Press, 2009), http://www.agassessment.org/.

3 D. Rieff, *The Reproach of Hunger: Food, Justice, and Money in the Twenty-first Century* (New York: Simon & Schuster, 2015).

4 Andy Fisher, *Big Hunger: The Unholy Alliance Between Corporate America and Anti-Hunger Groups* (Cambridge, MA: MIT Press, 2017).

5 Karl Polanyi, *The Great Transformation: The Political and Economic Origins of Our Time* (Boston, MA: Beacon Press, 1944).

6 Thomas Piketty, *Capital in the Twenty-First Century* (Cambridge, MA: Harvard University Press, 2014).

7 M.A. Altieri, *Agroecology: The Scientific Basis of Sustainable Agriculture* (Boulder, CO: Westview Press, 1987).

8 Steve Gliessman, "Defining Agroecology," *Agroecology and Sustainable Food Systems* 42, no. 6 (July 3, 2018): 599–600, https://doi.org/10.1080/21683565.2018.1432329.

9 La Vía Campesina, *Declaration of the International Forum for Agroecology*, https://viacampesina.org/en/

declaration-of-the-international-forum-for-agroecol
ogy/.

10 J. Pretty, *Regenerating Agriculture; Policies and
Practice for Sustainability and Self-Reliance*
(London: Earthscan Publications, 1995). N. Uphoff,
*Agroecological Innovations: Increasing Food
Production with Participatory Development*
(London: Earthscan, 2002).

11 Peter Rosset, "Cuba's Nationwide Conversion to
Organic Agriculture," *Capitalism, Nature, Socialism*
5, no. 3 (1994): 20.

12 United Nations FAO, "Trade Reforms and Food
Security: Conceptualizing the Linkages" (Rome.
Food and Agriculture Organization, 2003), http://
www.fao.org/docrep/005/y4671e/y4671e06.htm.

13 United Nations FAO, "Declaration of the World
Food Summit on Food Security" (Rome. Food and
Agriculture Organization, November 2009), www.
fao.org/fileadmin/templates/wsfs/Summit/Docs/
Final_Declaration/WSFS09_Declaration.pdf.

14 Declaration of Nyelení, Vía Campesina, Selingué,
Mali, 2007. https://nyeleni.org/spip.php?article290.

15 EHNE-Bizkaia, "Food Sovereignty in Practice in the
Basque Country," *Food First Backgrounder* 19, no.
3 (Fall 2013).

16 Frances Moore Lappé and Joseph Collins, *World
Hunger: Ten Myths* (New York/Oakland: Grove
Press, Food First Books, 2015).

17 Steve Brescia, *Fertile Ground: Scaling Agroecology
from the Ground Up* (Oakland, CA: Food First
Books, 2017).

18 Peter Rosset and Miguel A. Altieri, *Agroecology : Science and Politics* (Black Point, Nova Scotia: Fernwood Publishing, 2017).

19 Eric Holt-Giménez, "Racism and Capitalism: Dual Challenges for the Food Movement," *Journal of Agriculture, Food Systems, and Community Development* (2015), http://dx.doi.org/10.5304/jafscd.2015.052.014.

20 Samir Amin, "Food Sovereignty: A Struggle for Convergence in Diversity," in Eric Holt-Giménez, ed., *Food Movements Unite! Strategies to Transform Our Food Systems* (Oakland, CA: Food First Books, 2011), xi–xviii.

21 IPES, "From Uniformity to Diversity: A Paradigm Shift from Industrial Agriculture to Diversified Agroecological Systems", International Panel of Experts on Sustainable Food systems (2016), www.ipes-food.org.

22 Pat Mooney, Chantal Clements, and Nick Jacobs, "Too Big to Feed: Exploring the Impacts of Mega-Mergers, Consolidation and Concentration of Power in the Agri-Food Sector," IPES – International Panel of Experts on Sustainable Food Systems (2017), www.ipes-food.org.